Taking *the* Reins

Let Horses Teach You to Lead with Spirit

Taking the Reins
Let Horses Teach You to Lead with Spirit
by Jean Starling

ISBN: 978-0-9795324-0-5
Copy Editor: Christine Frank, www.ChristineFrank.com
Cover & Interior design: Toolbox Creative, www.ToolboxCreative.com

⁓ Acknowledgments

Thank you to my husband and best friend, Cliff Scutt. Without his support this book would not have been possible. He showed unwavering confidence in me during this new venture. He also took on all the daily horse chores that come with keeping and maintaining four horses, from feeding and cleaning stalls, to keeping them brushed, allowing me the time I required to write and rewrite this book. When I would have spent too much time in front of the computer he coaxed me into taking walks and getting much needed fresh air. In the final stages when the pressure was on to complete this work he even took over cooking our meals to ensure that I was eating healthy food. I could not ask for anyone to be more supportive than he has been and continues to be.

To my daughters Beverly, Angela, Tammy, and Elizabeth for the many episodes of "what do you think of this"? A special thank you to Angela who, when she received my frantic "I need help" calls, managed to fit me into her already very busy life. Thank you to Linda Kelbert, Marianne Dodd, Richard Bailey, Debbie Desoer, Susan Wright, Roma and Roy Gerle for taking the time to read this book and give me feedback on how to make it better. Thank you to Michelle Robinson and Elaine Cortez for their personal support during this process. Thank you to

Melinda and Marianne Dodd for last minute copy work for this book.

Thank you to the staff at Everett Community College for participating in my very first workshop with horses and for all your enthusiastic feedback.

A special thank you to all the horses I have learned from and love. Each one that I had to sell was difficult for me. I finally decided that running a breeding business was just too hard because I always had to say goodbye to horses that I loved.

I want to say a particular thank you to Jan B. King of eWomen Publishing Network. When I called Jan and told her I had an idea for a book, I had no idea what to expect. As an unknown writer with an unpublished memoir, I was unsure of myself and my abilities. I had never met Jan, but she immediately took time to listen to me and encourage me to proceed with my new idea. Over the next few months when I felt as if I did not have the talent or knowledge to write this book, she continued to encourage me and tell me that this was a worthwhile venture. Without her consistent encouragement, help, and pushback to do better, this book would not have been written. Jan, I owe you much more than I could ever repay. Keep up your work, you are needed.

Taking *the* Reins

Let Horses Teach You to Lead with Spirit

⌒ Introduction of Horses

Minnie - An 8-year-old black quarter horse mare

Karma - A 10-year-old blue roan quarter horse mare

Dee - A 4-year-old sorrel quarter horse mare

Rocky – A bay quarter horse gelding

Tasha - A 3-year-old black bay quarter horse mare

Halle - A 3-year-old black quarter horse mare

Snickers - A 2-year-old bay roan quarter horse gelding

Cupid - A 4-year-old blue roan quarter horse stud

Joe – A 4-year-old bay quarter horse gelding

Paint – A paint gelding

⁓ INTRODUCTION

You might be asking yourself what horses have to do with learning to be a more effective leader. Big, beautiful, and powerful, they see through any polite or political masks that we might attempt to hide behind. Sensitive and intuitive, they mirror-image back to you the feelings and emotions that you have hidden deep within, including those that affect your abilities as a leader. Working with horses provides the opportunity to learn by doing. They give you the chance to practice your leadership skills and when you make mistakes they forget and forgive almost instantly, never holding any grudges or remembering past mistakes. They are quick to respond to your new learned skills and behaviors, making them the perfect feedback loop for how you are progressing in your leadership growth.

With more than twenty years in corporate America in management, consulting, and training, I was looking for a new stress-reducing hobby. My love for horses coupled with my entrepreneurial nature led me to quarter horse breeding and performance showing more than ten years ago. Working on a daily basis with mares that had babies by their sides and watching them grow from young horses into adulthood I began to learn leadership in a new way. Though

I had many years of leadership experience and classroom education, the lessons from my interactions with my horses were coming faster and deeper than they ever had from the classroom. With their ability to see through any incongruent behavior on my part they insisted that I learn my leadership abilities better and in a new way if I wanted to accomplish my goals with them.

As an instructor in leadership, communication, personal and professional development skills, I began to see the possibilities for helping others grow and learn in this new, faster way: this new way of learning that sticks. I began holding workshops and coaching sessions to teach others these new lessons using my horses as a medium for learning. The results of this experiential method, using simple exercises shared with a highly responsive, beautiful horse, is exceptional and lasting. Following my intuition brought me here, where I write this book to share some of the insights that I have gained from these experiences.

Working with horses taught me Inspirational Leadership, leadership that seeks to inspire others by who you are as well as what you do. Large, powerful animals, horses can easily overrule you if you attempt to dominate and use force. To lead a horse you must convince the horse that he wants to do what you, the leader, want him to do. Leadership, when you strip away all the layers, is really about your ability to inspire others to follow you: Follow-ship. When you think of Leadership as being the ability to inspire follow-ship, then the question you must ask of yourself is, who do I need to be and what skills and abilities do I need to inspire others to follow me? Skills and abilities can be learned and being who you desire to be is about personal development. Becoming a great leader is about developing your self and your skills. Before you can help others grow, you must know yourself and take the time to develop into the person that you yourself would want to follow.

Leadership is a prevailing topic and an essential need. In our increasingly smaller and more complicated world, we need exceptional leaders more than ever. We have many books on the topic of leadership because the subject is deep and wide, so deep and wide that not one book can cover all the aspects of great leadership. Each of us who writes about leadership writes from our own perspective and in a way that is unique for us and therefore unique for you. Each one of us draws on our own experiences and from who we are to bring you many and various ways to view leadership and leadership skills. We give of our beliefs and of ourselves in our writing, so while some of the attributes of leadership may be the same they are delivered differently and you will hear them differently. You will therefore learn in a new way, the way that is right for you, the reader.

This book is written in the form of stories. These stories are of simple interactions with horses. They come from a variety of sources: my personal work with my horses, observing my husband Cliff, and workshop participants. In each of these stories I share leadership insights observed from these interactions. I have included the insights after each story so the flow of the story was not interrupted. I wanted to share my insights on leadership of self and others but I anticipate that you will gain your own insights as you read the stories. That is the wonderful thing about stories as metaphors: we each come with our own set of life experiences and filters therefore you may get something entirely different from the stories than the insights I have shared. It is my hope that you will enjoy and become more skilled in leadership of yourself and others from this book.

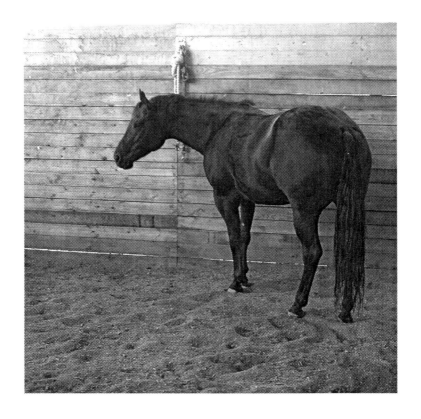

Minnie

CHAPTER I

Inside the Stable

⌒ KNOWING YOURSELF

Being a successful leader is as much about whom you are as what you do. It is necessary to look deeply into yourself and evaluate what you find there. Ask yourself the why questions that lead you to personal growth. Think of yourself as having three levels:

The conscious—where we process facts, analyze problems, recognize our feelings, and show ourselves to the world. At this level we are aware of our experiences while we are experiencing them.

The subconscious—is where we store information and what makes us react to a given set of circumstances, while sometimes unaware why. In our subconscious we may remember information we read, the mood of a piece of music, or how it felt to do a flying lead change.

Our Spirit—Our spirit is what drives us to improve ourselves; to love, trust, and make commitments. It includes the attitudes that lead us to act as we do and determines what information and experiences we seek out. In our spirit is where we are touched by the beauty of a horse running in the field or standing grazing in the pasture. Here is where we are inspired to grow and become. It is in our spirit that we learn from horses how to be a more effective leader and person.

The thoughts, feelings and emotions that live in our conscious, sub conscious and spirit governs our body. Our body and our energy react to these thoughts, feelings and emotions sending off messages to those we are around.

In order to inspire follow-ship it is necessary to balance these three levels. Our subconscious and conscious mind as well as our spirit needs to be in inner harmony and alignment.

⌒ When I Settle They Settle

Minnie is sleek and shiny black with eyes that dart left and right so that she can watch my every move. She is standing stiff and tense by the round pen wall, waiting for me to begin our workday. Her ears are turned towards me and her eyes are wide, showing the white around the pupils. She looks like she is ready to bolt for the slightest reason. Today is a foggy, rainy day with the air just cool enough to require me to wear a coat; when Minnie sticks her nose out to blow and snort I can see the air as it rises and circles from her nostrils and finally dissipates in the wind. The atmosphere feels heavy with some unseen expectation hanging, waiting. Her tenseness surrounds us like a dark cocoon and I find myself waiting for one of us to snap like a banjo string.

Picking up the whip I point it at Minnie's hip and before I can say a word, she springs up in the air and jumps forward, racing around the arena. Frustrated I think the word *whoa* and as I let my breath out to say the word she slides to a stop. I point with the whip again, this time asking her to change directions. She bolts with her tail in the air galloping around and around the arena. Her breath in the cool morning air continues to rise, circle like smoke, and then dissipate. Once again I barely think the word *whoa* and she jumps to a stop. Her whole body jars and bounces with her stop and it appears that she will come up over the top of the round pen wall.

I am feeling more and more agitated. What on earth is wrong with her today? This is getting us nowhere. Throwing down the whip and grabbing the lead line I lead her out to the pasture mumbling the whole way. *I'll just let her work off her excess energy alone*, I mutter to myself. When I let her go Minnie races about fifty feet into the pasture, stops, looks around, and then quietly begins to graze. It seems she has no excess energy now!

I have two other horses to work, so, shaking my head, I head up the hill to the barn. Dee is a little red mare with a white blaze down her face and three white stockings. Her mane and tail are the color of corn silk. She has big, wide, quiet eyes that belie the energy and athleticism she has in her body. She is very flashy and fancy-looking and I expect her to have a long show career. Her hocks are strong and she can move exceptionally slow but she is also so athletic that she can actually buck while running up hill. She will be able to perform multiple events on the quarter horse circuit. She is two years old and occasionally attempts to treat me as if she were the lead mare. She is quiet today, but pushes her nose out at me to tell me to get out of her space. Tapping her on the shoulder to tell her to stop it, I halter her and lead her out to the round pen.

Beginning our work with free lunging allows her an opportunity to move around the pen without any pressure from a line and tells me what her attitude is before we get started on anything else. So I unsnap the lead line to begin our work and before I can even speak she races off, rears up on her back legs, jumps into the air and starts bucking around the arena. She runs around and around the pen rearing, bucking, and snorting. Each time I ask her to whoa she screeches to a halt just long enough to turn and jump into the air, twisting and heading in the opposite direction.

Allowing my temper to get the best of me I yell at her to whoa and head out of the pen leaving her inside to work off her energy alone.

Funny thing, when I leave she settles down and trots over to the side of the pen so she can watch Minnie in the pasture. Mumbling and frustrated I flounce into the house, pour a cup of coffee for myself, and head out to the covered viewing room to see what they are doing. Now that I've had a few minutes to calm down and I'm sitting watching Minnie peacefully grazing in the pasture and Dee standing longingly watching Minnie, it finally dawns on me.

This is about me today, not them. Horses mirror-image their handlers. If they are bouncing off the walls it is because there is something in me that is bouncing off the walls. They are reading me; it is my energy that is causing them to exhibit high, uncontrollable energy. I am the one who needs to take the time out and figure out what is going on inside me before I can get anything accomplished with the horses.

INSIGHTS:

Dig deep to inspire follow-ship. While I could have forced the actions based on my role as leader, to inspire follow-ship requires a deeper commitment and work beyond simply performing an assigned role. Rather, it requires a leader who leads from the inside out. The only way we can lead from the inside out is to be aware of and mange the thoughts, feelings, and emotions originating in our subconscious mind. It is in the subconscious mind where thoughts and emotions begin to take shape. These thoughts and emotions carry both positive and negative energy, and energy communicates with those you desire to lead. Left hidden, unmanaged, and raw, this energy will sabotage your leadership efforts. Inspired follow-ship at the highest level can only be achieved when your inner person and your outer person act as one. Effective leaders not only prepare their spoken word but also prepare their subconscious to effectively lead.

⌒ RIDE BAREBACK

Sandy pulls the blue mounting block next to Bell and then moves to her head, holding her steady for me to mount. Bell turns her head to look at me. Her eyes are soft and liquid and seem to bore into my soul. Keeping my eyes on hers I glide my hand over her neck and shoulder. I want her to know that everything is okay. This is the last exercise in our workshop and the group has offered me an opportunity to step out of my role as leader and participate.

Floyd Cramer is playing quietly on the stereo and the atmosphere is serene and peaceful. Taking hold of Bell's hair on her withers I pull myself up and onto her back. She is not wearing a saddle so when I get on I have to adjust myself so that I am sitting in the middle of her back. Sandy is at Bell's head holding onto the lead line. Angie is standing at Bell's left side with her hand on my left leg to steady me and Lisa is at Bell's right with her hand on my right leg. The goal is to make the person on the horse feel safe and steady because in this exercise we will be led around the arena bareback with our eyes closed. I have facilitated this exercise many times, but now being the one on the horse I am struck with the trust that I am placing in Sandy as the leader and Lisa and Angie to make sure I do not slide off Bell.

Closing my eyes I lean over and place my open palms on Bell's shoulders, letting my fingers lightly pat her skin. Sitting quietly and taking a deep, relaxing breath, once more trust is uppermost in my mind. This feels like living trust and I am surprised at the slight tightening in my stomach. I can feel Bell's sides as she breathes in and out and the rhythmic movement reminds me that she and I have a relationship built on love and respect. I relax, knowing that Bell will take care of me, but in this instant I realize that giving my trust has to be a conscious decision on my part and one that is not always easy for me to make. Letting go of the reins and allowing others to be in control is difficult for me.

Sandy has been patiently waiting while I have been sitting here musing about trust. Bell is standing quiet waiting for her cue to walk.

"Okay, let's go."

Sandy clucks to Bell and tugs lightly on her lead rope and Bell begins to walk off. I can feel every step Bell takes and my body moves with each step. With my eyes closed it's harder to keep my sense of where we are in the arena. I can count each step Bell takes: *one, two, three,* and *four. One, two, three, four,* the rhythm flows through my body. I feel in balance and the feeling makes me smile involuntarily. Two or three more strides and my body is out of balance, with my pelvic bone rubbing uncomfortably on Bell's shoulders. Adjusting myself I am in balance again. My "aides" are quiet so the only noise is Bell's feet softly landing on the sand in the arena and the thoughts in my head.

It feels like Bell and I are alone in the world as we travel around the arena with me finding my balance, keeping it for a few strides and then losing it again. I finally get it! I have been attempting to be in balance 100 percent of the time and feeling as if I were failing by not achieving that. But balance is a moving target. Life is always in flow. The key is for me to realize the importance of balance and to continually move to meet my balance point. Becoming out of balance is just a step in the rhythm of life and being aware of that rhythm and flow allows me to move to gain my balance once more.

INSIGHTS:

Great leaders are lifelong learners. Being a leader who can inspire follow-ship requires leaders who are always learning and improving themselves. Life is a series of rhythms and, like the rhythms in a classical music selection which crescendos up and then comes crashing down, our life forces go up and down and are forever changing. We never stand still. We are either moving forward to meet life's changes or we are sliding backwards as life moves around us.

It is important to put ourselves in situations where we will become more aware of our own issues and expand our own boundaries, not only for ourselves but also for those we lead. Talking about trust was easy enough for me to do, but when I put myself in an experiential environment that required me to trust I found that talking about trust and living it were very different. As a leader who wants to be the best I can be, I now am aware that trust is an area that I need to work on personally. The only way we continue to grow and become a great leader is by expanding our own personal boundaries.

Balance, like life, ebbs and flows. Being in balance is a critical component for being an effective leader. But an effective leader does not need to be a perfectionist. Effective leaders know that balance will ebb and flow so they move and grow with life and continually rebalance themselves to meet the needs of the individuals they lead.

Sylk

⌒ Get Quiet and Listen

Sylk is docile today, with her big soft eyes quiet and watch-ful. She looks exceptionally pretty with a white blaze that runs down her face in contrast to her red- gold hair. Her body hair coat is glowing red-brown with the lights from the arena glancing off her coat. She seems to know that her work today is going to be quiet and relaxed. As I walk her into the arena with the workshop attendees watching, she glances up at them in the viewing room and seems to say *don't be afraid, I am here for you*. The energy she gives off is peaceful and serene.

We have covered all the basics of safety and horse interactions and now the attendees, a group of leaders from a local business, are ready for our first exercise of the day. In this exercise I want to have each participant center himself and check in with their body, taking the time to listen to what it has to say.

In working with my horses over the last several years I have learned that our bodies are extremely intelligent tools. What we may have stuffed inside ourselves far away from our conscious minds our bodies have stored waiting for us to listen to it. I have found that the more I work with the horses, the more I have the ability to listen to my body and the more I trust what my body and my intuition tells me. When I have not taken the time to listen, the information comes out in a variety of ways, some of them not when, where, nor how I would like.

Being outdoors with the horses and experiencing rather than being in a classroom listening to a lecture is very powerful. Today with Sylk's help I want each person to listen and learn to trust their own bodies in a safe environment. They will be able to take the first step by accessing the information and feelings their body has stored rather than listen to the thinking mind that chatters all the time.

Therefore I work with one person at a time in the arena where we take a few minutes to slow the process of life down and check in. I allow Sylk to roam freely during this exercise and watch her to make sure that her actions are safe for the person in the arena. With quiet music playing in the background I ask each in turn to breathe deeply; access and feel each area of their body.

With each participant, unseen forces are at work and my intuition reveals to me thoughts, feelings, and information about the person. As if on call Sylk moves in close to the person and goes right to the area in their body that seems to generate more intense energy. This intense energy is the area where they either have some physical pain or are holding onto some hidden emotional pain. Though we are relaxed in our sessions the exercise is powerful and our emotions run high. Several times we choke back our tears when their energy speaks to us.

The rest of the group watches quietly when it is another's turn. The only sound you hear is the music softly playing in the background and Sylk's footsteps when she walks over to the person and puts her face right at their energy level. Sylk acts act like a sensor for areas of energy and emotion that each has closed off and refused to hear.

Later, when we have completed the exercise, we spend time debriefing. Talking about emotion and energy as communication precedes a lively discussion about negative energy and the undercurrents of tension they have had in some of their group meetings.

"I walked into a meeting last week and the air was thick with negative energy," Josh contributes

"Were you able to tell where the energy came from?" I asked.

"Well, no, I couldn't tell."

"How do you know it wasn't from you?"

"To tell you the truth, I never thought about it until now."

"Now I realize it could easily have been me," Josh thoughtfully adds. "Without taking the time to know what I was keeping hidden, I guess I wouldn't know whether it was my energy or theirs"

"I am sure there have been occasions where I have thought it was someone else when it was really me," Kathy contributes.

The rest of the group chimes in and we talk about how important it is to become aware of the hidden emotions and energy in our body. Our day is done and we are all tired but excited about what will come the next day.

INSIGHTS:

Your body sends you messages. Routinely, our bodies send us information that we have long since forgotten in our conscious minds. Our bodies store emotions, events, and energy and will send us this information when we get quiet and listen. It might be a remembered feeling that tells us we have been in this emotional space some other time. It might be a tenseness around an individual or action that reminds us we have felt this feeling before. If we listen carefully we will have the information we need to tell ourselves how we want to act in this new situation based on our success or failures in dealing with this same type of issue in the past. Our bodies are highly intelligent tools that we need to respect and listen to for success in leadership.

Our emotions are energy. Each and every day we are surrounded by energy. The atmosphere has energy and each of us carries energy in our emotions, at both the conscious and subconscious levels. To be an effective communicator and leader it is imperative that we tune in to this energy. To really communicate and lead effectively, we must be able to distinguish what is our energy and what is others' energy. Others will sense our energy. If our energy is self-confident and peaceful they will respond with confidence in us as a leader; on the other hand, if our energy is intense and unhealthy they will respond in like. Though they may not be able to understand what the feelings mean, they will know whether they are comfortable with us or not. Only by recognizing and managing our own emotions and energy will we be successful in inspiring follow-ship.

⌒ Muck Out Your Own Stall

Dee is playfully galloping around the arena. Racing to the far end to the wall and back again she bucks and rears straight up in the air. The sky is dark, with huge, angry, wet clouds and it is pouring rain. When Dee has excess energy she loves to run it off and the only opportunity she will have today is in the indoor arena. I am giving each horse free time in the arena alone so they can run and play and release their energy.

While Dee works off her excess energy I am getting some paperwork completed. Done for the day she walks over to the side of the arena by the viewing area where I am sitting and looks up at me. Her big, soft, blue eyes are wide-set, showing her quiet, intelligent nature. Her eyes question me but, getting no response, she relaxes and stands near the wall just below where I am sitting.

Dee is a two-year-old filly that I bred and raised. We have spent many hours together. One of the exercises that she and I enjoy is jogging beside each other in the arena. I will attempt to keep up with her as she trots or lopes around and she loves the play that we have together in this exercise. Often as we play she begins to act as if she thinks of me as another horse and will kick her feet out at me to attempt to take the leadership role. I know that she would like for me to "come in to play" but today I don't have the time. Standing by the wall Dee has become frustrated with waiting for me so she walks off kicking up the dust in the arena with her feet like a bored child who hasn't gotten what she wanted. She picks up the whip I have laying in the arena as she walks off and flips it around with her mouth and over her head.

"Can you be the leader of me?"

I clearly hear her say as she walks away.

I ignore her challenge and decide to go to the barn and clean her stall while she is out. In the barn I push the gray wheelbarrow up to her door and begin picking out her stall with the red manure rack.

Over the last few weeks the horses have been edgy, nervous, and spirited when I work with them. I have found myself feeling the same way and I am not sure if it is they who are affecting me or me affecting them. I do know that I have come to a standstill in my life. After twenty years of working and building a career I have hit a wall. While I know that I need to move forward and continue to use my leadership abilities I am stuck and feel as if I have nothing more to offer as a leader. My work with my horses is the only thing that is keeping me grounded, so I find myself spending more and more time with them. Knowing that something is going on inside me that must be resolved but not sure how is the thought that is uppermost in my mind today. I am musing about this while I am mucking out Dee's stall.

Like a burst of light in my head, all of a sudden words in rhyme start flowing through my mind. My mind is doing leaps and bounds with words coming so fast I cannot keep up. From never reading poetry to it's flowing through my mind too fast for me to even keep up is a surprise to say the least. I am not sure what is happening but something inside me insists that I go back to the viewing area and get the rhyme down on paper. Almost running I head back out to my pen and paper. I write page after page, with most of the writing about the horses. I am not sure how poetry is supposed to be written but it does not matter at the moment. When my hands are too stiff and cold from the damp air to write anymore I reluctantly quit for the day.

Dee in the meantime has been wandering around the arena watching me or just standing in the corner waiting. Both of us are done for the day so I lead her in to her nice warm stall. She's quiet and peaceful, content and ready for her food, as if she has accomplished her task for the day.

While I am working with my horses over the next few days, something inside me pushes its way to the top and painful memories that I had suppressed bubble up and come to the surface. My writing takes a new turn all on its own and I find myself writing about my life as a child in the south, poor and fatherless in a family of nine. Almost before I know what is happening I am catapulted into writing about the episodes in my life that brought fear and hurt. I realize that these episodes have driven me in each and every decision I have made with no awareness on my part that I was being driven and certainly not of what was driving me. The next four months my waking moments are spent writing until at last it seems that I have written what I needed to write for "The Story."

Being with the horses in the peacefulness of the outdoors and in a moment of quietness my intuition had spoken in such a unique way that there was no denying what I was supposed to do. Had this spontaneous knowing come in another, less direct way, I might have ignored it. But coming in this way it left me no choice but to follow its lead.

Now I realize that my leadership abilities needed to be honed in order for me to move to my next level. I could not become the leader that I needed to be without first learning to listen and trust my intuition much more completely. My intuition gave me my first assignment, which was to face and understand how my hidden fears, hurts, and emotions had and were driving my outward behaviors. Next I needed to heal. Writing my "story" was a part of my healing process. To move forward to my new leadership roles required me to prepare myself at a deeper level.

INSIGHTS:

Follow intuition, the flash of information and knowing that comes from your body, mind, and spirit. History tells us that our greatest leaders listened and trusted their intuition. This best friend who has no other agenda than to make us successful whispers in our ear and gives us the complete information and guidance. A leader's ability and willingness to access, trust, and use her intuition will make the difference between mediocre leadership and highly effective leadership. Tuning in to your intuition takes practice but is your secret method for inspiring follow-ship.

Buried pain lives on. Few of us are without histories that do not include hurt, pain, or fear in one form or the other. It is having lived and endured these hurts, fears, and pain that give us the ability to reach others on an emotional level. That is, if we have not stuffed our feelings inside and never taken them out in the light of day. Hidden fears, emotions, and hurts will drive your outward behaviors. We must heal ourselves to help others heal and as a leader who wants to inspire, it is your emotional connection that gives you the ability to reach those you want to lead. It is not a selfish act to take the time to heal your past hurts. Rather, to reach your highest potential as a leader, it is imperative that you first heal yourself.

⌒ Mind Speaking Rope Twirling

Snickers is swishing his long black tail impatiently at the flies that are swarming around him. Our horse sitter suggested his name to us because he looks like a Snickers bar. He is very tall, with long legs that are black with a few white hairs in the mix, and reminds me of a tall, graceful dancer. A young horse, he is balanced even at this age and has strong legs and hocks. He can lope from a standstill with no apparent effort whatsoever.

I am just beginning to teach him how to respond to stimuli around his back, legs, and hindquarters. I want him to learn to stand quiet even if something should accidentally startle or fall around him. I have a white lead rope that is about fifteen feet long that I use specifically for this exercise. Hooking it to his halter which has a snap just under his chin I can hold him and work with the end of the lead line at the same time. The end of the rope has a piece of leather about five inches long. This gives me a way to make it snap and make some noise if I need to get him to focus.

Holding onto the rope I twirl it around and around, making circles with it over his head. I twirl it close to his left side and then his right side, just barely missing touching him with it. I want him to see the rope moving around first before he feels it. The noise and watching the rope twirl around and around makes him nervous so he jumps from side to side trying to get away. Paying no attention to his skittish movements I focus on talking soothingly to him and keeping the rope moving at the same time. After about ten minutes he trusts that the rope is not going to hurt him. While he is still not happy about it's twirling around him, as evidenced by his wide owl eyes, he stops moving around and for the most part stands quiet. We have made it through the first step.

Next I begin to throw the end of the rope over his back. His back is the color of Oreo cookie ice cream and my mind wants to drift to food and lunch so I have to get refocused before I lose his attention. Throwing the rope over his back first from the right side and then moving him around me by backing him up a little and moving his head around to my right, I throw it over his left side over and over again. After I spend a few minutes doing this he begins to stand quiet and watch me. In my mind all I have been thinking is *stay quiet and easy.* Verbally I am saying "Easy, boy, nothing here to be afraid of, don't worry, it's okay." With my mind staying quiet and thinking quiet thoughts and my mouth saying the same thing, my body responds and stays quiet as well. He hears my soothing tone and feels the quietness in my body and begins to lose any idea of moving away from the rope. I know that he gets it and is beginning to get desensitized.

We have completed our desensitizing exercises for the day but now I want to work on having him move away from the rope when I twirl it around his hip. The actual physical act of twirling the rope doesn't really change much. To get him to move away from the rope I twirl it around and to the side of his hip. I twirl the end of the leather, not touching him with it unless he gets locked up and does not move at all. The difference is that now I expect him to move his hip away from the twirling of the rope, where before I wanted him to stand still.

I know that whatever is in my mind transfers to my body and that he will read my body language. Therefore I stop and stand still for a few minutes, centering and readying myself for the mind change. Snickers is standing with one leg cocked up and yawns lazily.

Once I have centered myself I take a deep breath and begin to bring my energy level up. In my mind I begin to think *Snickers, move your hip over* as I twirl this rope and then I begin to make "smooch, smooch" noises with my mouth. Not too happy about being disturbed, Snickers sends scowling looks my way. I allow my mind to become more energized by being more alert myself and letting my thoughts move faster and faster. My body immediately responds and I stand a little taller and move my arm a little faster. I don't want to scare him; I just want him to move over so I carefully balance the energy in my mind and body. As I think it my body does it. He senses the change in my body and I can see his body tense as he begins to shift his hip away from the rope. Standing on his right side and keeping my mind and body with focused energy, I ask him to move his hip over to the left and then I move him around once more so that I can ask him to move his hip to the right. Over and over again we repeat this exercise until he moves smoothly and quickly away from the rope. Now that he understands the difference in being desensitized and being asked for a maneuver we have completed our work for the day.

Insights:

Thoughts and feelings create intention. Intention creates action. The thoughts and feelings that begin in your subconscious mind are the driving force behind your actions. Let's say you are a manager in an organization and you have been asked to stay late tonight and talk to your team about some upcoming organization changes. You may not understand or agree with the changes yourself or you may have a favorite television program that is coming on tonight and if you delay you will miss it. Either way, your actual intent is to get the conversation over with, not to spend the time to help your team understand and support the changes. Your true intent of just getting it done is what your team hears and will respond to. This is lack of intention in action. It's like saying you are going to make a certain number of sales calls. The sales calls become the real intention rather than actually making a sale. To be an effective leader you must practice true intention rather than activity and be honest with yourself in regard to your true intention. Your teams will know the difference and will be guided by the intention rather than the activity.

A successful leader will keep his subconscious and conscious mind in alignment, practicing true intention. When practicing true intention, the body believes what you are saying and communicates that message. You begin to make it happen.

⌒ Open the Gate to Reflection and Self-Honesty

Dee is like a cat ready to spring. Her ears are cocked forward, alert and listening. She watches intently as Lois, one of the workshop participants, walks into the arena. The rest of the group is silent, watching. The wind picks up speed, picking up a plastic tarp that is sitting just outside the arena and blowing it against the arena wall, causing it to crackle in the silence. Dee jumps and begins to race around the arena, running back and fourth two or three times before she realizes that nothing is after her and settles down. But she stands alert, ready to take off for the slightest reason. There is a consistent scratch, scratch as the wind blows stray branches up against the side of the arena. Although these external factors are causing Dee to be jumpy I know that there are other reasons as well.

Lois's body is stiff, her face white, anxious, and agitated. Though I do not know what is causing Lois to generate so much high stress and electric energy, I decide to use it in this next exercise. Her task: halter Dee and walk her to the end of the arena to the group. Holding up the halter and lead rope I explain to Lois how to put it on Dee's head and buckle it.

Lois takes the halter and walks towards Dee. Letting her get about three feet away Dee takes off running and bucking to the other end of the arena. Dee is so athletic that when she runs and bucks she is a sight to behold for sure. I can sense Lois getting more anxious watching Dee run and buck. She swallows hard and heads after Dee again. This time Dee doesn't even let her get close before she takes off again. Lois barely contains her frustration as she heads after her. Dee has decided that no way is she going to let this woman catch her. So she runs away again and again. It is definitely time to help Lois out.

Taking the halter from her I lay my hand on her shoulder and guide her to turn her back to the group. We are at the far end of the arena so they can see us but can't hear what we are saying.

"Breathe deeply, now exhale slowly"

"Once more, now one more time and this time let your whole body beginning at your shoulders drop down, releasing the tension, and blow your breath out."

When I know that her body is more relaxed I continue on.

"Is there anything bothering you?"

With what is supposed to be a smile but doesn't quite make it she answers.

"Oh you mean like maybe the huge argument I had with my teenage daughter this morning about lying to me."

"Or maybe the pressure my boss is putting on me to get a report done by tomorrow night."

Having said what was on her mind Lois's body is more relaxed but I still sense something deeper is bothering her. Contemplating the situation I decide to ask her to attempt the exercise again, knowing that she has yet to reach full authenticity.

Dee has ceased her running and bucking. She is more comfortable with Lois. But when Lois walks over to her this time she walks away. While she is comfortable enough to stop running she is not comfortable enough to allow Lois to halter her.

Lois looks at me with her frustration showing on her face.

"Lois, let's peel the apple to the core."

"What do you mean?"

"My process improvement adage is to ask the question five times."

"By the time you ask the question five times—peel the apple to the core—you will have gotten down to the, in this case, subconscious level."

"In other words you will get to what is truly going on at your core level."

"I see," She answers a little nervously.

"So let's go down one more level to the core."

"What is really going on?"

With tears in her eyes Lois tells me she is no longer happy in her role at work. She is not sure what to do about it yet but it is now clear to her that she has to do something.

Having voiced what is really bothering her, her body now visibly relaxes. Her body is now completely relaxed and she gives me a warm smile. She is now ready to be truly authentic.

"Are you ready to go get this spooky horse now?"

Squaring her shoulders she smiles her answer and heads back towards Dee with the halter in hand. This time when Dee acts like she is going to walk off, Lois moves in to head her off. Dee allows Lois to halter her and lead her down to the group. She has completed her task.

INSIGHTS:

Wise leaders know that authenticity begins at their subconscious level. Being who you are and being honest with yourself is the only way to practice congruent behavior. Your subconscious and conscious minds need to be in sync. Only then will your body and your verbal speech be congruent and authentic. Others know when you are not being authentic and they respond with confusion. You are sending them mixed messages. Effective leadership requires authenticity. You will always have internal dialogue and conflicting emotions. But it is when you attempt to hide these emotions from yourself rather than verbalize and deal with them that you become incongruent. By verbalizing your emotions you can release the tension that surrounds them and become more congruent in your body. The conflicted issue may not be resolved, but by bringing it to the surface and acknowledging it you have released the power it holds over your subconscious mind. You can now deal with it and resolve it where before it stays hidden and becomes bigger with each passing day. Great leaders will practice peeling the apple to the core by asking the five questions of themselves, their team members, and the processes they lead.

⌒ Gain Confidence in the Saddle

Tasha is tall, dark bay, elegant with big hips and a short back. Her shoulders are upright and when she moves she looks like she might have been told by her mother to stand up straight, put your shoulders back, and don't slump. But of course she wasn't; she exhibits natural self-carriage. Cliff says she looks like you would expect a horse to look and everyone who sees her agrees with his assessment. All who see her assume that she will be a top western pleasure horse. But even though she has natural self-carriage we have to teach her to carry a rider, with her body rounded up and slow so that she carries herself and her rider in a slow collected trot and lope that is a pleasure to see and a pleasure to ride.

Hence today in our training we are going to work on self-carriage by doing exercises to teach her under saddle to carry herself and me in the proper frame. After I have warmed her up by putting her in the round pen and free-lunging her we are ready to get started. Climbing on her back I trot her over to the large outdoor arena. I want to use the arena fence as a straight line to work her on. First I walk her down the rail and back up and then, turning her around, I lay my hands on her neck in front of the saddle horn. This ensures that I will not accidentally pull on the reins by mistake. I want her to trot on the rail on her own holding her body upright and exhibiting self-carriage. Trotting her down the rail I allow her to trot on her own with no help from me. She is able to trot twenty feet or so before she begins to veer off the rail and gradually edges to the inside of the arena. Each time she veers off I take my hands off her neck and take hold of the reins to pull her back over to the rail. Once there I put my hands back on her neck and continue to trot her down the length of the one-hundred-thirty-foot arena and back up again. We continue with this exercise for about thirty minutes and by the end of our time she is holding herself over against the rail for longer and longer periods of time without help from me. We will work together each day on this exercise until she is able to hold herself on the rail at the trot and lope.

As the days go by she progresses by exhibiting self-carriage and she begins to gain confidence in herself and her abilities. After a couple of months she has enough self-confidence and self-carriage to be able to complete the exercise on her own.

INSIGHTS:

I have been a student of human nature for many years and a student of horse behavior, movement, and personality for more than ten years. I've watched people in many different environments and foals from the time they are born into being a full-grown horse. One outstanding observation has been evident. When one of my horses exhibited self-carriage with or without self-confidence, rather than proving they could do it, they had to prove they could not. Just the way they carried themselves would cause people who saw them to expect them to succeed. If they did not look the part people did not believe they could do it. Conversely, the horses who did not exhibit self-carriage had to prove they could be a good western pleasure horse.

With people I see the same conduct. If "Sharon" exhibits self-carriage, people around her expect her to sound and be successful. If she does not talk with confidence or exhibit successful behavior they are surprised. Watching others in leadership roles who do not exhibit self-carriage, I have noticed that it is more difficult for them to lead with respect, connection, and trust even though they hold the leadership role. You only have to look at some of our political candidates to see this in action. The candidates may have almost identical credentials but usually the one who will win the race is the one who exhibits self-carriage. Self carriage is essential to inspiring follow-ship.

Many years ago when I was first learning to teach leadership and management I took several train the trainer courses. In these courses we had a saying: "Fake it till you make it" Surprisingly it worked. Now years later I can expand on that some. Now I add, if you do not feel self-confidence in your given situation then fake it till you feel it. I'm not suggesting that self-confidence is not important. I'm offering that when you first begin something new, it is almost impossible to have self-confidence in your ability to do it. But if you have self-carriage your demeanor says to others: *respect me; I am a force to be reckoned with.* Then by continuing to do the thing you will gain confidence in your self and your ability. You will feel it and your self-esteem will rise. Self-confidence is important to your continued success as a leader but you do not always start out with self-confidence so build on your self-carriage.

Dee and Sylk

CHAPTER 2

Horse Sense

⌁ Knowing Others

True leadership is serving others and caring about their needs as much as your own. The only way to fulfill this commitment is to study and understand others. Review their personalities and understand what they need in order for them to grow and become all they are meant to be. Leading others is an honor and requires a loving approach. When using this approach you will find that people will respond quickly with trust, energy, and performance.

Become a
People
Whisperer.

⌒ Speak in Whispers

Minnie is striking beautiful as she stands in the round pen today watching us. She is a six-year-old quarter horse mare that we bred and raised. The workshop attendees love looking at her with her jet- black coat shining in the sun. Her job today is to walk and jog in the round pen listening and obeying as each participant commands. This seems to be a small task, one that can easily be accomplished.

Joel steps into the pen, striding quickly to the center of the circle. His movement and actions are forceful, direct, and to the point. He knows what he expects from Minnie and by the determined set of his shoulders he plans to get it done and get it done quickly. As an aid and extension of his arm he is allowed to use a whip but his instructions are never to touch Minnie with it.

Minnie lays her ears half way down as she warily watches him.

"I wonder who he is and what he wants."

"Hold on, he is moving way too quick for me."

"Oh no, he is going to hit me with the whip. I better get out of here fast!"

Minnie has begun to race around the arena to get out of Joel's way. She is not listening to him as he attempts to slow her down.

"Why is he yelling at me?"

"Uh-oh, he is going to catch me and he looks mad. I better run faster and stay out of his way!"

By now Minnie is wildly galloping around the pen with Joel frantically trying to get her to slow down. His whole body is moving back and forth as he waves his arms trying to get Minnie to stop.

"Here he comes again, he looks like he is going to beat me," Minnie is screaming as she comes to a sliding stop.

"What do you want?"

"I'll do whatever you want, just don't hurt me."

Minnie is releasing her breath in ragged spurts and her stomach is heaving.

I know its time to bring Joel out of the round pen. He looks totally bewildered and not at all sure of what has just happened. His composure is shaken and he steps out of the pen shaking his head. He doesn't say a word as he takes his seat.

After a short break our group is once more at the round pen with Minnie now standing sleek and relaxed by a shade tree just on the other side of the pen. Her back foot is cocked up and her eyes are half-closed. Dennis is up next and he is clearly a little nervous after watching Joel with Minnie. Dennis quietly walks to the center of the pen but you can see it is a struggle for him not to wander over to touch and caress Minnie first. The rules are no touching for this exercise so he holds himself back and instead reaches for the whip. The rest of the group is exceptionally quiet, almost as if they were holding their breath waiting to see what will happen.

Minnie senses someone in the arena and wakes with a start. Her eyes open wide and the whites of her eyes show around her eyeballs. She is clearly wary but she stands quiet waiting to see what this person wants.

Dennis makes a half-hearted attempt to get Minnie to trot around the pen but his actions are more words than actual intent and Minnie easily senses this. He fumbles with the whip and swings it back and forth to get Minnie to move. Watching him all the time, she continues to stand under her tree. He begins to coax her, trying to get her to move. Dennis doesn't seem to know how to confront Minnie and be firm in his requests for her to trot. After a few minutes of his asking and her refusing to move, he drops the whip to the ground and is done with the exercise.

INSIGHTS:

Know how your style affects others. We are each born with a unique personality style and while we change as we mature and learn, we maintain a uniqueness that is ours alone. While researchers have developed useful methods to group certain personality traits and behaviors it is important to note that even within these categories we are each still unique. That being said, it is essential for leaders to become aware of their leadership styles and their effect on those they lead. Each style has strengths and weakness and while a leader with a dominant style might be successful with one team he may need to adapt his style for another team.

Each individual will respond to your leadership efforts according to what they are comfortable with. One person may like a fast pace and instructions given on the fly while another will want to sit down and take notes and get more detailed information before they attempt your request. A more left brain person will want to have information given to them in a sequential pattern as you would find in an outline. The person who is more right brained will take in information more in the spatial mind mapping style and get bored very quickly if you attempt to give them all the details before they have a grasp of the big picture. Attempting to lead each individual with the same method is like a horse trainer who has one way and wants to train each horse with this same method with no allowance for the individual needs or differences. Only a leader who is confident within himself will be flexible enough to adapt his style to meet the needs of those he leads. When a leader is unsure of themselves they may become rigid and lack flexibility because they are actually running on fear that they may not be the leader they are expected to be. Learning new methods and gaining self confidence is necessary to be able to lead with flexibility.

Wise leaders are aware that knowing whom you lead is essential for effective leadership.

⌒ Each Horse is a Different Color

Minnie, Sylk, and Dee have been brushed and groomed
until they shine. We have a workshop today and each horse
has a role to play. It's obvious from the way they act that
they are feeling very pleased with themselves. After all,
they got an extra brushing today and plenty of hay to eat
and are just hanging out in their stalls.

Minnie is a six-year-old black quarter horse mare with
a beautiful head and big, expressive eyes. She has no white
on her at all so when she is loping around the pen what
you see is refined elegance in a package that reminds me of
Black Beauty.

Sylk is also a six-year-old quarter horse mare but
she is a golden-red color. She has a white strip on her face
and while Minnie is more refined, Sylk tends to be built
stockier.

Dee is a two-year-old quarter horse mare who is a
deep red color with three white stockings, making her look
like she has on white socks. She has a wide white blaze
down her face with wide expressive eyes. She is the most
athletic of the three and the smallest, standing at only about
four feet, seven inches.

Sandra has chosen Sylk to work with today, so we
halter her and lead her out. Minnie and Dee let out a
nicker as we leave with Sylk, which I am sure means they
are laughing at Sylk for being the first one to have to go to

work. Sylk's main joy in life is eating so I am sure she would much rather stay in her stall next to her friends and eat. But that is not on the agenda for the day.

As soon as we put Sylk in the round pen and remove her halter she immediately begins to jog around the perimeter of the pen without even being asked.

I can hear her thinking, *The sooner my work is done the sooner I can get back inside to my hay.*

Turning to Sandra I instruct her: "Ask her for a lope, then jog and walk"

Sylk does her job and looks like the show horse she is with her reddish-gold hair coat shining in the sun and her body rounded up and collected in her gaits. Sandra looks at me like *Wow, this job is easy.* Sylk is in her zone and for a few laps around we just leave her alone. Then, listening to my instructions, Sandra moves in front and to the side of Sylk's shoulders to get her to change directions and go the opposite way. This is an exercise that I use to get the horse's attention on me. Sylk jumps up and twirls around, now loping in the opposite direction. Sandra looks at me and raises her eyebrows, questioning me. I ignore the question and continue with my instructions.

"Let Sylk go ten feet or so in one direction and then ask her to reverse and go the opposite direction"

Sandra has to run to keep up but gets her body in place in time to ask Sylk again and again to change directions. Each time, Sylk jumps around and lopes off with her ears back showing her irritation. Her body is stiff and unyielding and though Sandra repeats the exercise over and over she refuses to settle in and just accept being interrupted and asked for something different than she has in mind.

"Now back off and let her go around the pen, allowing her to move at whatever gait she wants to."

When we leave Sylk alone she goes back into her zone and is quite happy to continue to go around the pen as long as we allow her to go in the direction and the speed she chooses.

As a team member, Sylk wants to be given the job and be left alone. She is uncomfortable when she is interrupted in her pace.

John is going to work with Dee so we bring her into the round pen and remove Sylk. Dee gallops into the round pen and the first thing she wants to do is get in our space. She wants to play with us as if we were another horse that she can nip and charge and be lead mare with. To get her going I snap my black whip and move her out to the edges of the circle. A little wild and free, she keeps pushing the boundaries trying to come back into the middle with us.

John mumbles aloud as to why he got this one to work with. Laughing, I give him the black whip along with instructions on how to get Dee out and working. After a few attempts he does get her out but only after he visibly takes charge. When Dee senses that he is not to be toyed with she settles down and listens to what he is asking her to do. She is very interested in what is going on over the fence with the mares in the pasture and time and again he has to turn her and get her to focus on him in order to complete his task. With the exercise completed we are ready to move on.

Dee pushes against the boundaries and is always looking to be the boss mare if given the opportunity.

David will work with Minnie. I paired him with her especially because his nature seemed calm and quieting. Minnie, the black spitfire she could easily be named, came bursting on the scene. To get us started off right I caress Minnie on her shoulders and ask David to do the same. Our goal is to allow her to feel safe and calm with us before we begin work. David matches my movements as we calmly move to the center of the pen.

Asking her to walk then jog and lope, David stays quiet in his movements and voice. Minnie watches him closely and quickly does whatever he asks her to do. Her body never quite relaxes and her movements are jerky. She begins to lick her lips almost immediately to show her submissiveness to him and to ask to stop. She clearly wants to be done as soon as possible. She rushes into each gait when he asks for them. She is so afraid of getting into trouble that she wants to make sure she does it and does it fast.

Although Minnie is a beautiful mover as well as being stunning to look at, she has never quite made it on the show circuit. She is ultra-sensitive to all her surroundings and to each small movement a person makes. Her thoughts are only to please but not to please for pleasing's sake but to please to make sure she does not get into trouble. These traits have made it almost impossible for her to relax and show at her best even though the few times she was shown she placed very well and even won futurity moneys. It is her mind that stops her from being the top pleasure horse we bred her to be. She has made a very successful brood mare and loves being a mother so that is her job on the ranch now.

Minnie is very inward-focused and performs out of fear for herself. She does what she is asked but is so consumed by fear and insecurity that she is never really able to relax. To help her be successful it is imperative to fit her to the right role and responsibilities.

David has been successful in getting her to do her job in the round pen. Our day is done.

Insights:

Become an expert on personality styles. An effective leader is a style expert. They will take the time and effort to study, recognize, and understand the different personality categories because in knowing these categories they will know how to approach and lead their teams. Each style has unique needs for their most effective learning and communicating. While each individual is unique in their style there will be many similar attributes. By knowing these attributes a great leader will be able to adapt to the learning style that the person needs. Remember, leadership is about reaching the individual and giving them what they need to be successful. The only way to achieve this is by knowing them.

Great leaders know that one size does not fit all and have the self-confidence and knowledge to adapt their style to the individual. Adapting is about being wise enough to be flexible, not about being someone who you are not. A horse trainer who believes that he or she can use the exact same methods of training on every horse is a horse trainer who has only a few horses to train. Each horse is different, therefore the trainer has to be wiser and smarter than the horse and be able to vary the methods to reach their goals. So much more so is the human diverse in their needs.

A true leader has the compassion and ability to look past the outer man to the beauty and potential within.

⟜ Beauty Is More Than Skin Deep

Rocky is standing in the center of his corral with his butt turned towards us. He is a big brown gelding with his back caved in as if he had permanently lived in a saddle for months on end. His body looks battered and beaten. We can hear his joints creak as he puts his weight first on one foot and then another.

Turning his head he glances our way more as a reflex than from any real interest in who we are or what we are doing here. His eyes are liquid pools of pain and sorrow. The despair there is so real it feels as if I have been kicked in the stomach. I caught myself just before I doubled over with the pain.

Sharon steps purposefully out from the group of women who have come for training.

"I know this horse."

"I want to work with him!"

My chest feels tight and I have to remind myself to breathe in even breaths rather than jagged spurts. I watch quietly not knowing what to expect from their interaction. The silence is so complete we can hear Sharon's jeans rustle together as she moves slowly into Rocky's field of vision.

He gives the barest flicker of an eye her way and then just stands in his corner as if she does not exist. He acts too tired, too beaten, too dejected to care. Sharon is in no hurry. She edges closer and closer into his space. When she is in his energy field he moves away, just a few steps but enough to say *leave me alone.*

Sharon backs away leaving him his space for what seems like hours but in reality is a minute, maybe two. Her eyes are full of love and compassion as she gazes into his face. The energy that comes from her body is so loving, patient, and kind that even outside the pen we can feel and sense the glow that she creates.

I am mesmerized by this poor, beaten old horse that has long since lost his external beauty and yet has the ability to inspire such love and patience from Sharon. I feel as if I am viewing a very private love scene and am honored to have this opportunity.

Twenty, maybe thirty, minutes pass with Sharon edging closer, Rocky moving away, and then Sharon following. They repeat this pattern over and over until Rocky finally stops, turns, and looks at Sharon with what I can only say is the barest hint of hope in his eyes.

"Maybe she does care, this woman who keeps moving closer to him."

"Maybe she will love me, honor me after all."

"I'll give this woman one more chance to show me that I do matter, that my life does mean something."

Rocky stands quietly basking in the aftermath with Sharon whispering softly, saying things for his ears only as she gently lovingly caresses his neck, shoulders, and flanks.

"Dear God, it feels good to have someone care about me."

I am reminded of watching an exposé on television of Princess Diana as she held sick, dying, and diseased babies and young children in her arms with no regard for herself. Seemingly no thought of the diseases these children carried that she might be exposed to and certainly never showing any disdain for the dirty and visually unlovely among them, her eyes full only of love, caring, and acceptance.

INSIGHTS:

Leaders who inspire committed individuals have love enough to spare for the lovely and the unreachable among us. True leadership sees through the rough, battered exterior to the beauty that lies within each individual and focuses on the beauty they find there. With their focus on the individual person, they take the time required to reach the most unreachable. Many of history's greatest leaders started out with nothing more than love and caring for the needs of one individual and then, because they gave their love and commitment to the one, they have inspired thousands. When a leader has the ability to see past the outer man or woman to the beauty and potential within, then they are able to guide the person to become more than they would ever have thought possible.

Leadership of self
is the first step
in the leadership
of others.

⌒ Keep Your Eyes on Your Herd

Lisa and Janice have come today for a coaching session. We will be working with Minnie. Lisa is the manager at a nonprofit agency and Janice is her friend who works in administration. The coaching session is more for Lisa as she is having some issues with being listened to and being taken seriously in her role as leader and manager. I am a little unclear what Janice wants to gain from the session but as we begin I start to understand her role.

Minnie is wandering around the arena waiting for us and Janice is immediately taken with her beauty. We are in the balcony talking before we get started and I can hardly contain her, she is so anxious to get down to Minnie. In the sunshine today Minnie looks very black and extremely elegant and a little bored as she looks towards us and then away.

"I wish they would hurry the process along."

"It is so warm out, I want to get out to the pasture and be alone for a while."

"Okay, here they come; wonder what they want of me today."

We have talked about some of the issues Lisa is having at work and I notice that Janice takes the nurturing role with Lisa, making sure that I understand what Lisa's problems are and explaining things for Lisa. I find the dynamics interesting since Lisa is the leader at work but she looks to

Janice to "go before her." Therefore Janice will be the first one to work with Minnie. Her assignment is to ask Minnie to walk and trot around the arena. The first thing she does is to pet Minnie and stand in front of her face even though I have asked her not to touch Minnie but to move her around the arena. By standing in front of her she has made it almost impossible to get her to move. She runs her hand down her face, then her neck and shoulders, soothing and petting and coddling. Minnie loves this; she does not have to do anything but just stand and be petted and look pretty.

"Wow, this is going to be easy today."

"This woman is happy just to rub me and it feels quite good."

"I wonder how long she will stand and rub me if I stand close to her and sniff her hair."

I make the decision to watch for a few minutes so that I can understand the dynamics of the relationships Janice forges and to see if she will complete her assignment with no interference from me. After a few minutes it is clear to me that the role Janice plays in her relationships is that of caregiver. She praises Minnie over and over; even though Minnie has yet to do anything but stand there. Janice really does not ask anything of her and yet is lavish in her praise and worship. Her expectations are low and she seemingly does not require much in response.

I let the scene play out before me for a short period and then remind Janice that she is to ask Minnie to walk and trot around the arena. Minnie looks like I have betrayed her.

"I wish she would just shut up!"

"We are perfectly happy just to stand here."

Janice finally moves away from Minnie and raises her arms up, concurrently raising her energy level, and motions for Minnie to walk off. Minnie lays her ears back and acts like she has been asked to compete in a pleasure event rather than just walk around.

"Okay, okay, I'll do it"

Janice gets Minnie to walk around and then jog before she allows her to stop. Once again she lavishes praise on her. Her style is clear to me and I spend some time talking with her about her successes and challenges at work and how she contributes to or hinders them.

She understands but clearly has no desire to make any changes. Rather she is ready to move on and support Lisa in her exercise. She takes the caregiver role once more and encourages Lisa to come down and begin her exercise.

Minnie and I look at each other, both of us wondering if we will be able to make an impact on these women today.

Lisa walks into the arena and begins speaking right away. She barely glances at Minnie but picks up the whip I have offered as an aid to get Minnie to walk off. Minnie laughingly looks at me as if to say *no way will she get me to trot, I recognize this style.*

Lisa barely hears anything I have to say as she continues to tell me what she thinks about her job, her employees, and employer. They do not listen, they do not respect her, and they do not want to change anything they are doing. I have to ask her two or three times to ask Minnie to walk off and then trot. She makes a couple of half-hearted attempts as she continues to tell me what is wrong at work. After ten minutes or so I see that she is clearly not going to get Minnie to do anything but stand on one foot and yawn. Therefore I take the whip from her and attempt to get in a few words so that we can process the experience. Clearly Lisa's focus is on herself and no one else. She is concerned for her needs only and cannot even stop long enough to hear anyone else's needs or desires. Janice feeds on and supports this behavior.

INSIGHTS:

A successful leader is other-focused. It is impossible to inspire follow-ship when your focus is only on your needs and desires. The individuals you lead will see through any selfish motives and know when your concern is for their needs or when the actions you take are meant only to fulfill goals for yourself.

While personal development is imperative for a leader, it is also imperative to focus on what others need to be successful. You can only be a successful leader if you have successful followers.

⌇ Train Both Sides of the Brain

Halle is grumbling while she wanders around loose in the arena.

"Why am I stuck in the arena today?"

"Sylk and Tasha have gone off to graze."

"I want to go!"

"When will you let me out?"

Occasionally she looks up at me with her big, dark eyes, whinnies, and then when I do not answer she wanders down to the end of the arena and back up again. Her black legs are long and lean, making me think of a ballet dancer. She has a slow walk but her stride is long and she covers a lot of distance easily so it doesn't take long for her to walk from one end of the arena to the other several times.

"Okay, okay Halle, come on."

I can't help but smile as I wave her in. Thinking she is going to go play with her buddies she comes trotting up to the gate. Moving in close to her shoulder I turn her head towards me and slip the halter over her head.

"Let's go, girl."

She is still expecting to go run with her friends so to get her more focused on me I lead her around the arena a couple of times. Then when she is quiet and listening to me I know that we are ready to begin work so I call workshop participant Johnathan in.

Spending a few minutes with him before we get started, I explain that I want him to accomplish three maneuvers with Halle.

1. Ask her to give her head laterally.

2. While giving her head laterally, move her hindquarters away from pressure.

3. Move her shoulders away from pressure turning her on her hindquarters.

First I demonstrate each move to Johnathan so that he has a visual picture of what I want him to accomplish with Halle. Halle's body is very flexible and these are exercises we have completed numerous times so when I ask her she moves almost automatically to complete each maneuver.

Next I hand Johnathan the lead rope and ask him to get Halle to give her head laterally to the left. Johnathan takes the lead rope, moves his body into position beside Halle's left side, and pulls the lead rope out and up to her back. Halle turns her head to her side giving him her face.

"Good, now let go of the pressure on the lead rope."

"The quicker you release the pressure after she gives to you the faster she gets the idea and knows she has done it right."

Johnathan smiles, visibly pleased the he has gotten Halle to bend her neck and give her head to him.

"Second step: now bend her neck around and get her to give to you and then ask her to move her hindquarters over at the same time."

Johnathan listens attentively and then asks Halle to give her neck and move her hindquarters over.

"This is fun!"

"Yes, it is fun when you are able to get them to maneuver when and how you ask them to."

"Now for the third step: lay the lead rope over Halle's neck, making sure there is no pressure on her face by allowing some slack in the rope."

"Keep Halle's head straight by touching her cheek lightly on the band of halter to hold her face."

"Then using your right open palm, apply light pressure on her side just behind her front leg. "

"But what about her head? It is in the way."

"Walk into her expecting her to move away from you."

"But what if she doesn't?"

"Well, are you applying pressure?"

"Yes."

"Have you taught Halle to move away from your pressure?"

"Yes."

"Then what do you expect her to do?"

"Move away from the pressure, I guess."

"Then ask her for the maneuver."

Johnathan put the lead rope over her neck and placed his left palm on her halter and his right palm at her side. I can see that he is applying some pressure, but as Halle moves over a little he fails to follow her with his feet. Sensing this, Halle stops and refuses to move even though he applies more pressure with his hand.

Johnathan frowns and looks at me. I want the process to play out so I wait for him to try again. Once more and when he gets the same response, he is clearly at a loss. So taking his place beside Halle I ask her to move off the pressure from my hands and expecting her to move I move my feet and walk into the space she leaves behind.

"Johnathan, can you tell me the difference in what I did and what you did?"

"The only difference I saw was that you walked almost into her shoulder as she was moving."

"So would you say that I fully expected her to move as I had asked her to?"

"Yes, for sure."

"Did you really expect her to move when you asked her to?"

"No, I guess I didn't, because if I had I would have walked with her as you did."

"So you got what you expected, right?"

"Yes, I did." He smiled

"Okay, so try again."

Johnathan asks Halle to move her shoulders around but this time walks into her fully expecting her to move around and she does.

"Whoo hoo," he yells

Giving Halle a rest I spend the next few minutes with the group as we discuss how these interactions apply to leadership.

Johnathan is very pleased with himself and begins to leave the arena.

"Hold up."

Puzzled, he looks at me.

"Remember a horse has two brains, one on the left and one on the right. You must train and lead both brains to get the whole horse.

"We worked Halle's left side and left brain but now we need to work her right side and right brain."

"Just because we train her left side does not mean that the right side knows what to do unless you train it as well."

Johnathan walks over to Halle on her right side and turns her head to the right but she is stiff on her right side and refuses to give to the right.

"Horses are like people: they have a tendency to be either primarily left-brained or right-brained; that is, stronger on their left side or right side."

I encourage Johnathan to get Halle to give her head to the right once more. This time he holds a little longer and she gives her head. Moving onto the next maneuver which requires her to move her hindquarters as well, Halle stalls out again.

Halle and Johnathan are both tired and Halle is getting agitated. Turning to the group I ask,

"Would you say that Johnathan and Halle have been successful today?"

"Yes," they all chorus.

"So should they push forward and work on moving the hindquarters today or back up and leave the exercise at a successful point for the day?"

"Back up!" they all chorus.

INSIGHTS:

Lead both sides of the brain. In order to train our horses we have to work with both sides of their bodies, doing the same thing to each side. Otherwise they will know how to move away from pressure on one side but not the other. Were we to teach them to move away from pressure on their left side and not the right, they would have no idea what we wanted on their right side. When we think of the human brain in this way it is easy to understand why we must train and lead both sides of the brain with individuals. A person who has the tendency to act and respond more from her left brain will need to see and hear information in a much more objective and sequential way. While a person who is more right-brain oriented will become bored and get lost in the detail if we present the information in this sequential pattern. Individuals that are more right-brained will need to hear and see information more as a whole pattern. It will be difficult for this type of learner to focus on the details until they can see the whole picture. This learner will learn in a more intuitive and holistic way and needs to be emotionally connected to the information. A right-brain learner will intuitively see the connections between leading horses and leading people. A predominately left-brain person will have more difficulty. You will find that people will fall more into a middle ground with using both sides of their brain but with a preference for one side or the other. It is imperative for your success as a leader to take both sides of the brain into consideration with your leadership efforts. In our programs we use methods to train both sides of the brain which ensures a more well rounded program and individual.

Give your team periods of rest. It seems such a simple thing, though one we often forget. To make the greatest progress towards a goal individuals need rest and relaxation periods. Just because it's simple don't forget this key component in your leadership planning.

Imagine you are excited about a goal and you and your team are making huge strides in reaching this goal. Everyone is on a high of sorts and the end is just within reach. Then things begin to fall apart, tempers flare, and your progress slows down. What do you do and what is the problem? Back up to the last successful event, and repeat this event if necessary. Help your followers feel good and successful once again and then give them rest. In our excitement to reach a goal as a leader we sometimes push too hard and push past our followers' pressure points. Some pressure is good but it must be balanced with rest. Back up, regroup, and take some time. You will find that when you begin anew you and your team will be ready to move forward once more with the huge strides to reach your goals.

Minnie and Dee

⟋ Ride with Forward Energy

The big white and brown gelding is standing in the middle of the arena with John, the featured clinician, on his back. From my distance on one of the top rows I can see that the horse is highly agitated and working himself into a frenzy. He jerks his head up in the air and then tosses it left and right. John has a tight hold on the reins and proceeds to pull back, causing the horse pain and anger. Attempting to get away from the pressure on the bit his front legs come up off the ground as if he will rear. Just before the horse goes up in the air John releases his hold on the bit and lets him rest.

I'm sitting with a crowd of over two hundred at a horse expo where we have the opportunity to learn more about horsemanship from some top trainers. John has attained great respect in the horse industry for knowing how to train horses and people to ride them properly, so I know that he has a reason for this demonstration. Sitting on the edge of my seat I am anxious to see what he is going to do next.

Having given the horse a chance to rest, John now starts tapping him on both sides of his belly asking him to go forward. The paint gelding walks and trots around in a circle, with John talking to him and us at the same time. John's hands are resting quietly on his neck in front of the saddle horn. The horse is now moving with a nice cadenced trot. His head is down and his feet are soft as they hit the ground. He looks balanced and attentive. I can see that

John is making hefty strides in getting him rounded up and driving from his hocks while staying well- mannered. John grabs my attention with his next comment.

"Don't ride with your brakes on!"

He is giving the gelding the go-forward cue with his legs, but has begun to pull back on the reins again, causing the horse to gape his mouth open and begin the fight with his head once more. The horse stops trotting, plants his feet in the ground, and refuses to move. John is giving him mixed signals, the go-forward and the stop at the same time. The poor horse has no idea what is being asked of him. I can hear him thinking.

"What does this man want?"

"Should I go forward or stop?"

Not wanting to cause the horse any more confusion, John stops pulling on his face, drops his hands, and lets him rest. He doesn't need to say more because the message is clear: Don't ride with your brakes on, else you go nowhere and all you achieve is confusion and anger.

Insights:

Leaders, when you give mixed messages it has the same effect as attempting to lead with your brakes on. When you ask your team to move forward but don't give them enough instruction or you are not clear in your communication you have hindered them in their efforts. When you are unclear yourself in which direction you want to proceed but attempt to lead anyway you will achieve confusion. Before giving the go-forward cue an effective leader will have a well-thought-out goal in mind and clear instructions on how to reach that goal.

CHAPTER 3

Corral Culture

～ KNOWING THE TEAMS YOU LEAD

Leading a team is one of the most enjoyable and challenging activities you will endeavor to achieve. We live in a complex and ever-changing world and the fastest way to accomplish your goals is having people work together. To lead your team effectively it is imperative that you understand team dynamics and the best methods for achieving high-performance teams.

Sylk

⌒ Recognize Signals

Dee looks golden in the afternoon sunlight peacefully grazing in the pasture with her head down. Karma is eating four or five feet away. With the advent of the cool evenings her winter coat has been growing so that from a distance she looks a little like a wooly bear. Minnie, looking black as night, is grazing on the other side of Dee.

The workshop attendees' assignment: watch and observe.

We don't have long to wait. Although we don't see or hear anything, Dee stops grazing, raises her head, and looks around. For a fraction of a minute she stands perfectly still. Then as if the earth were going to open up and swallow her if she does not get out of the way she takes off running with her tail in the air. She lets out a bellow as she runs into the arena and over to the far side by the gate to the barn, snorting and blowing all the while. Startled, Karma and Minnie jump, then immediately follow Dee, galloping to keep up with her.

All three are standing at the gate with their tails in the air, snorting. Looking around to see what has caused the commotion I see the neighbor's kids out jumping on their trampoline. They are laughing and jumping and have no idea they have just caused the horses to spook and run off.

The horses have had a few minutes to calm down and see that nothing is going to hurt them so they are slowly and cautiously walking back out to the pasture to eat.

I have been keeping an eye on the group as this episode has unfolded and their faces show surprise and wonder at how fast the scene has changed before them from an idyllic setting with horses grazing peacefully in the pasture to all-out galloping to get away from an unseen danger. Since I want the group to really think about what we have observed I start asking them some questions.

"Did anyone see what spooked the horses before they began running?"

Looking at each other they shake their heads *no*.

"When did you see the kids on the trampoline?'

"Not until after the horses were in the arena at the gate," Julie offers.

"How did the horses know that something was out of sync?"

"They sensed something that we did not see," Bob responds

"Natural instincts of self-preservation!" Jim proposes.

"Yes, you are all right." I nod in agreement and we spend the next hour discussing instinct and its importance in leadership. As we spend time talking I share with them what I have observed in my work with horses versus people.

"Horses live instinctively in their right-feeling brain. They react before they think. In training our horses we attempt to get them to stop and think before they instinctively respond to unseen dangers. "

"People, on the other hand, are usually quite the opposite. In general they spend the majority of time in their thinking brain and need to use more of, and trust, their instinctive brain."

The group is listening attentively and Gordon pops up. "You know we spend so much time in our life not listening to our instincts. As a matter of fact I know that I have talked myself out of listening to my instinct many times and instead listened to my linear brain, only to find out later I would have made a much better decision had I listened to my instincts."

Concluding our morning session I respond,

"So the lesson then is to learn that our instincts are valid information in our decisions. This information is to be listened to and evaluated just as we would any other valuable source of information. But since we have spent so much time not listening, each of us will need to become more sensitive to hear our instinct and to learn to trust it once again."

INSIGHTS:

Just like Dee's, our bodies have built-in sensors. These sensors alert us when we are about to walk into danger or make a mistake or if there is something amiss in our environment. We do not need to think about it. This instinctive reaction comes to us automatically. Our problem begins when we allow our thinking brain to talk us out of this knowledge. Webster defines it this way: "make a complex and specific response to environmental stimuli without involving reason, behavior that is mediated by reactions below the conscious level." As leaders we would do well to learn from the horses and listen to our instinctive responses to a person or situation. There will be episodes where thinking before responding is a valuable reaction to have, just as there will be occasions when it is best to listen, respond, and ask questions later. Only by tuning in and using your instinct will you learn to trust, believe, and know when to respond without questions or when to question. Instinctive and intuitive information is the secret weapon of wise leaders.

Horses are herd animals and always have a leader. When their leader instinctively responds they do not stop and ask why; they simply follow suit. They have learned to trust their leader regardless of the situation. An effective leader knows that once your "herd" trusts you as their leader, they will instinctively follow your lead under pressure. This offers huge benefits in reaching your goals.

⌒ Deal with Distractions

Sylk looks red-gold, like the color of fall leaves, as she races around inside her corral. She runs to one end of the corral and then rears up as she turns around and races back to the other end. She is causing such a commotion it is hard to focus on anything else. I have three outside corrals that butt up against the round pen, with the round pen being in the center of the corrals. When I want the horses to be outside but not out on pasture we will put them in these corrals. Usually this works fine with no real problems. They stand in their corrals and watch when I have another horse in the round pen working.

Today having them close to the round pen is not working out too well. Tasha, my tall brown bay two- year-old mare, is on one side in her corral and each time Halle goes around the perimeter of the round pen and gets close to Tasha, Tasha will lay her ears back and lunge out at Halle. She is letting Halle know that she is not welcome in her space. With her ears back and lunging out at Halle, I can say this is one of the only times I have thought Tasha unattractive. She looks mean and nasty and if she could get to Halle I am sure she would kick out at her. Tasha is still young enough that she thinks she needs to challenge all the horses for the lead role.

Snickers is in the other corral that butts up against the round pen. A one-and-a-half-year-old quarter horse gelding, he is black, white, and brown-colored and looks amazingly like a Snickers bar. His temperament is usually quiet and pleasant, but today each time Halle jogs past his corner of the corral he rushes over with his ears laid back looking for a fight.

Halle has begun to race around the pen like a black bombshell. Rather than getting any work accomplished with her I am spending my time getting after the other horses and attempting to get them to stop their unruly behavior. My mood is a little down and I feel tired and agitated with little patience for their uncontrollable antics today.

I am feeling more and more frustrated with Tasha and her attitude, so rather than spending my time working as Halle continues her race around the pen, I decide to put her away and get Tasha in the round pen. When I put her in the round pen, she immediately begins to race around one way, then rear up and turn on her haunches and head in the other direction. When I try to get control of her by turning her around and around until I have her attention she lays her ears back and pushes her nose out at me. She is challenging me each time I ask anything of her. She wants to be the dominant leader today and wastes no time or energy in letting me know it. Snickers continues to race up to the corral fence by the round pen and lunge out, now at Tasha. He is also trying to establish his dominance. After a few more minutes of this I stop and go outside the round pen and sit down in a white patio chair I have outside the round pen. Clearly we are not going to get much accomplished today.

I sit thinking about the horses' rowdy actions and try to decipher the cause. I can force the horses to work but it will take twice as long to get anything done and in the process neither they nor I will be very happy. Now that I am sitting down and reviewing what I am feeling and what the horses are doing I begin to become acutely aware of how dark and gloomy it is out today. If one horse was out of whack I would think maybe they were just having a bad day. But when all of them are acting this way and I become more aware of my own moodiness, then I have to look at what else might be the cause.

Now paying attention to the environment around us, I feel the heaviness in the air and realize my body feels pressed down and lethargic. The sky is cloudy and overcast and the air just seems to hang heavy and wet in the atmosphere. It is the beginning of fall and this is the first day in months that we have not had sunshine. All I really want to do is curl up with a cup of nice warm hot chocolate, a warm butterscotch cookie or two, and a good book. Watching the horses I realize that indeed it is the atmosphere that has them all tense and irritable today. Since we have no immediate work we have to accomplish today, I decide to give them and myself the day off. I know that tomorrow we will get much more done and that a day off will be in all our best interests.

INSIGHTS:

An unfriendly atmosphere impedes your efforts. An unfriendly atmosphere can be a dark and stormy climate or a tense mood that emits from you or someone in your group. It can be tension and stress in your environment. The key to being an effective leader is to be aware of the environment as an input to the leadership and communication process and manage this input just as you would any other outside input. While positive stress can be a benefit to reaching your goals, negative or unfriendly atmospheric stress will have the opposite effect.

Successful leaders know that a break will often be the most effective strategy and get more results on the way to reaching their goals.

⌒ Form Partnerships

The thunder of hooves draws me to the window to see what is going on in the pasture. Just as I get to the window Sylk streaks by in a full gallop. I barely get a glimpse of her golden red-brown body as she races past. Thrusting my feet into my boots, I hurry out to see what is happening.

Horses are herd animals so they always want to be with another horse and Sylk is a mare that is especially herd-bound. Meaning when I take her away from the other horses her behavior becomes highly agitated. When she can't see the other horses she gets very upset, therefore I am pretty sure things are all right. But I decide I'd rather be safe than sorry. As I round the corner of the house, Sylk thunders over to the fence. She is racing so fast that I am afraid she will not be able to stop and will come crashing over the top of the fence. Just as she gets to the fence she comes to a sliding stop, so close that her chest comes within an inch of touching the fence rail. Her chest is already wet with sweat from running and screaming. Glancing around I see what the problem is. Tasha and Halle are in the pasture next to Sylk but they have gone down to the other end and she can't see them. I know that I need to move her or she will continue to race around and work her body into a sweat.

Walking over to the gate I take the halter down and hold it up for Sylk to see. She runs over to me, more than ready for me to take her. Walking her over to the adjoining pasture I turn her in with Tasha and Halle. As soon as they see Sylk they come over at a gallop.

Standing at the gate watching them, I am struck once again with herd dynamics. Even though Sylk can't stand to be alone, the first thing she does when Tasha gets near her is twirl around in a circle almost jumping in the air and kicking her back feet out at her. Tasha knows enough to stay out of her way and, pinning her ears back, she runs off. Halle makes sure she keeps her distance from both Sylk and Tasha. When Tasha and Halle are out together alone Tasha is the lead mare and if Halle acts in the least like she might challenge Tasha then Tasha will back up close to Halle's shoulders and kick out at her. Halle, knowing her place, will get out of the way. But when Sylk comes into the pasture she exerts dominant behavior and lets Tasha know that now that she has arrived on the scene, she is the leader. Once the pecking order is established they all three head out and begin grazing on the pasture.

I bred and raised Minnie, my other black quarter horse mare, and Halle. I have spent many hours watching them grow from small foals to young fillies and now mares. While Tasha wants to be herd boss, Minnie and Halle have no interest whatsoever. There seems to be a natural driving force within some horses for that leadership role while in others there is no desire at all.

INSIGHTS:

Understanding your herd is a must for effective leadership. Observing my horses in their herd, while different from the teams I have led, I have nonetheless noticed many similar qualities. Just like horses we are born with the need to socialize and interact both at work and at play with others. The psychologist

Abraham Maslow, in his theory of five levels of basic needs, ranks social needs as number three in his hierarchy right after the physiological and safety needs. Once a person has met the lower level physiological and safety needs, higher level needs become important. The first of these are social needs. Social needs are those related to interaction with other people and include:

- Need for friends
- Need for belonging
- Need to give and receive love

As a leader it is important to note that individuals in a team will spur each other to new peaks in their personal and professional growth. When I was learning to snow ski I found that if I skied with someone who was much better than I then I progressively got better and pushed myself more. When I skied only with beginners like myself I did not progress nearly as fast and did not feel the need to push myself. These are not new concepts but ones we frequently forget. It is important to allow for social and professional interaction. Teamwork, brainstorming events, and simple interaction time have huge benefits for personal growth and team growth. Online we even find master-mind groups. Even those who have chosen what might seem like a solitary career path find that they need professional stimulation. Even the simple act of the right pairing of individuals could help your team reach their goals faster and better.

A few years ago one of my daughters was going through her adolescent years and I had grounded her from her friends for two weeks due to some misbehavior on her part. She stayed in her room for days on end, barely eating or talking. She slipped into such a depression that I believe I found an acceptable way to shorten her restrictions from her friends because I was actually worried about her state of mind. When isolated for an extended amount of time from their herd or friends, a team member will spend their time and energy focused on getting back into the team rather than on the goals at hand.

An effective leader will plan for and encourage interaction between and among individuals in their teams.

But team or herd knowledge goes further; successful leaders know that when an individual joins a new team it will cause the team to go through an adjustment period where all roles will go through a redefining. This phase in a team is called the storming process and will happen in all teams before the forming of the new team roles and the norming.

In Maslow's hierarchy, once all the basic needs are satisfied, then the instinctual needs for self-actualization are activated. Maslow describes self-actualization as a person's need to be and do that which the person was "born to do." "A musician must make music, an artist must paint, and a poet must write." In my herd of horses I see this with the horses who have the desire to be the leader in the herd. They are born with the desire to lead and as they grow you can see it in their antics in the pasture. They are always pushing for the leadership role. If the "old" herd leader is sold or moved to a new herd the horse that has shown the drive for the leadership role will immediately establish herself as the new leader. Even if the established herd leader does not leave the herd, the horse who desires that leadership role will continually push up against the established leader. Observing my herd of horses I have seen them change leaders many times. Much of the time I have not been privy to the final episode that established the new leader, but with horses force and dominance are sometimes a factor. Others of my horses have shown no desire to be the leader and are happy in their roles as a follower.

Understanding team dynamics is an essential element for your success as a leader.

Leadership
is as much about being
as it is doing.

⌒ Move with Engagement

Dee, my little red mare, is standing with one foot cocked lazily eyeing me while I stand at the entrance to the arena watching the rain persistently pouring down.

It's dark out even though it is the middle of the day and Dee and I both are feeling lethargic and not in the least like working. Dee has her eyes half-shut and keeps herself just focused enough to know when I move away from the door. Since neither of us really feels like working I decide instead to exercise her and myself by jogging side by side around the arena.

Letting her jog freely I use my body as the vehicle for instruction. I motion with my hands for her to jog and I keep tempo beside her as we jog around and around the arena. Sometimes just when I least expect it I'll get a flash of intuition from my time with my horses and today was to be one of those days.

As Dee and I jog around we have moments of being completely in sync. We are headed in the same direction, of like minds; our bodies are almost as one, connected it seems at the soul level. The moments are fleeting, one minute in sync and the next one not. If I shift my focus even slightly we lose the flow. My body and mind feel the connection and I know in these connected moments that we can achieve great things. With no emotional space between us we move as one. The energy when we are in sync is exhilarating. The feeling each time we lose the flow is one of almost physical pain.

I know in a flash of insight that this feeling of being in the flow is where great leaders achieve great things, but the flow, like balance, is one minute there and the next gone. My goal with Dee had been one of exercise. Now the goal is one of learning to stay more consistently in the flow where as leader and led we move as one.

INSIGHTS:

Being in the flow allows for greatness. Have you ever heard an athlete recounting a story of a successful play? A singer after a successful concert? Or a dancer who has performed at her peak? If so, then you have probably heard the excitement and happiness in their voice as they recount flow. While they may not use the same words they are communicating the same feeling, the feeling of being in the flow. In the flow is that feeling of being at the top of your game where the world seems to be smiling on you and everything is working together at the right time and in the right way to complete the maneuver or dance or concert or whatever it may be in a wildly successful way. This is flow! Great leaders look for this same flow. When a leader and their team are in flow and in sync they are completely unstoppable. While being able to maintain this flow 100 percent of the time is unlikely, nonetheless great leaders will strive to obtain and stay in the flow with their teams as long as possible. Because they know it is at this level that the greatest challenges are met and the greatest connections are made.

CHAPTER 4

Horse Whispering

⌒ BUILDING TRUST AND CREATING RELATIONSHIPS

For a leader, becoming a horse whisperer is about reaching the highest level of trust and relationship with your followers. In this stage of your leadership growth you begin doing the things that build deep allegiance and inspire followership. You could be called a People Whisperer. A leader that individuals want to associate with because they trust and believe in you, who you are, and what you represent.

Tasha and Snickers

⌒ Doing the Groundwork

Sylk is yelling and pawing at her door. She's impatiently waiting with her head down for me to halter her when I slide her stall door open. A big, stocky, reddish-brown mare, she thinks I am going to put her out to pasture so when instead I cross-tie her in preparation for saddling she twitches her ears with obvious displeasure.

Picking up the curry comb and brush I spend a few minutes brushing her. She loves being brushed so she stands quiet and relaxed, her eyes soft showing her enjoyment. I am not only cleaning her hair coat; I am also building our relationship while I am brushing her. I talk to her and caress her shoulders and back while I brush her. She acts as if she knows what I am saying as I spend time telling her about my day.

After saddling her I lead her out to the round pen arena. The round pen consists of twenty six-foot high by twelve-foot long aluminum panels that we have shaped into a round pen for the purpose of exercising and training our horses. She is six years old and has had consistent training since she was two, but regardless of her age or how much time we have been together nor her many years of training, the procedure is always the same. Before we can begin work I must get her attention. Horses are constantly looking to be with their herd and always looking around to see what scary thing will come at them next. Therefore an exercise to get their attention is always the first step in our work.

Taking her halter and lead rope off, I send her out to the edges of the round pen by using my whip as an extension of my arms. The whip is a four-foot-long black plastic about one-half- inch in diameter with a long piece of black flexible nylon attached to the end. Using the whip allows me to get in front or behind her without getting so close that she could kick me if she chose. Asking her to go first one direction and then change direction at my command, forces her to focus her attention on me rather than what might be going on in the pasture beside us. With Sylk I know from experience that it takes a good ten minutes of this exercise before she is quiet and ready to focus on me.

So today I begin our session by sending her out to the perimeter of the round pen. I don't really care whether she is walking, trotting, or loping as long as she is listening to me. Sylk is feeling a little frisky so she begins loping around the arena to the right. I let her go four or five strides and then I turn her around by positioning my body and the whip just slightly in front of her. Pinning her ears in irritation at being asked to change directions, she slides to a stop and jumps around to go to the left. We complete this exercise over and over again until after a few minutes she slows down and is ready to trot on my command.

We have some success but we are far from finished with her exercise.

Sylk is a horse who likes to avoid; she is constantly looking for a new way to avoid or rebel. So believing that she has done as she has been asked she begins to look for a new way to control the exercise herself. She gradually begins to edge off the round pen wall, getting closer and closer to the center which reduces the amount of work she has to do. If I allow her to continue edging in then she is effectively doing half the work I am asking her for. So I push her shoulders out with the position of my body and the whip forcing her to stay on the round pen wall. I have to push her shoulders out with the whip several times before she knows that she cannot get away with cheating me.

Now as I ask her for the trot, turn, trot again we begin to get a rhythm. This works for a short time and then Sylk decides she knows enough to do it on her own and can decide when to turn around and trot in the opposite direction. While running to catch up with her, as soon as she turns on her own with no direction from me I force her to turn back and wait for my leadership.

This exercise is designed to not only get her attention but to gain her respect for my leadership. Horses always have a leader. Out in the pasture another horse may be the herd boss or here in the round pen it is me who is exerting my leadership, but with horses there is always a leader and the led. If I do not assert myself as her leader she will assume she is the leader and do as she chooses. This could certainly be dangerous for me in our work.

When she licks her lips and turns her eyes towards me I know that she is finally ready to respect me and accept me as her leader for the day. Asking her to stay on the perimeter of the round pen I walk over and caress her shoulders and tell her she is a good girl. Next I ask her to follow me around the arena by connecting with her both verbally and by touching her shoulders and then slowly walking away. When she follows me with no force on my part she shows me that we have connected and that she trusts me to lead her. I still have not put a halter on her. I want her to follow me because she respects and trusts me, not from the force of a halter and a lead rope.

I will have to follow the same regime tomorrow and the next day and the day after, being consistent with her each day. No matter how many days this week we ride our process will be the same. If I stay consistent the time it takes each day will get less. But though the methods may change the underlying process stays the same. To be safe and accomplish our goals each day I need to get her attention, make a connection with her, gain her respect, and build a trusting relationship.

It is not enough to ask her once and think that will be sufficient; instead I will need to ask each and every day. If I try to short-cut the process we will just stall out in our work. I may think that I will save time by skipping this step, but indeed the opposite is true. It takes more time to get our work done so consistency is essential.

Insights:

To inspire follow-ship in a world that is on information and activity overload, obtain the attention of those you seek to lead. Once you have their attention, in order to keep their focus you need to connect with them on an emotional level. Connecting on an emotional level ensures remembrance and real connection rather than a superficial passing. To keep connection you must build a trust relationship. The only way to build trust is by being trustworthy. Being trustworthy means others know that you will look out for their best interests. They can trust you because you are consistent and predictable in your interactions with them. By keeping your interactions with them predictable regardless of your moods or emotions they always know what to expect of you; they feel safe putting their belief and trust in you. One who is not predictable in their interactions keeps their followers on edge, never knowing what to expect. It is impossible to build and maintain trust with an unpredictable leader.

Respect is defined as high or special regard and is absolutely essential as a building block to your success as a leader. Respect is showing a balance between firmness when needed and flexibility and is never given to a leader who does not first have respect for herself.

A wise leader knows better than to assume that "because I followed you today I will automatically follow you tomorrow" without your asking for the leadership role each and every day with a variety of methods and behaviors. Building a relationship is not a one-time interaction, but consistent, trusting interactions.

Snickers

⌒ Buck Up

Minnie, looking a little bored, is standing on the side of the arena with her foot cocked up in back waiting for us. She is in no rush to get going this morning and yawns and stretches her back up and her front left leg out. I am sure she would like to simply doze in the sun and not be interrupted today with work.

She will partner with Sharon, a young college student, who has come out today to experience this work more as information for a class she is taking than for any real need of a coaching session. Sharon has grown up with horses and has spent several years showing on the American Paint Horse Association breed circuit. I am not quite sure what to expect myself this morning since Sharon has extensive experience with horses and has not indicated any thing in particular that she wants to work on. My stance: a wait-and-see and let the session go where it will.

Sharon needs little instruction on lunging Minnie so I just stand back and watch. Sharon begins lunging Minnie and for a couple of minutes things go fine but Minnie quickly senses something in Sharon and decides that indeed she does not need to work today after all.

"Cluck, cluck, cluck." Sharon snaps the whip and continues clucking to Minnie to get her to trot. Minnie trots about half a circle and just stops. Sharon snaps the whip and gets her going again. Minnie lazily trots off, goes a few steps, and stops again. After a few more attempts Sharon shows her frustration by simply staring at me like *how do I get this mare to trot*. This is not what I had expected so, being careful to hide my surprise, I walk in closer to them and casually ask:

"How is school going for you this semester?"

"I am taking some required subjects, so not as interesting as it could be, but I am very busy."

"Have you made new friends this year?"

"Yes, some"

"What about boyfriends?" I continue to probe.

"Well, I have a long-time friend who is now a boyfriend but he does not want anyone to know about us!"

The words and story start to tumble out of her mouth. She shows her hurt and lack of understanding of her situation in her face and body as she tells me her story. Her boyfriend does not want any of their friends to know that they have a relationship so they are keeping it a secret and have been for months now. He is away at another university so they talk on the phone and see each other on weekends. As we talked Sharon couldn't come up with why they were keeping it a secret other than he just wanted it that way. For some reason he was uncomfortable with their friends knowing about them. Red flags are going off in my mind as she talks.

"How do you feel about keeping this secret?"

"I hate it, and I have told him that we either come out in the open with it or I am breaking it off."

Sharon is close to tears as she responds. Her face is flushed and her whole body shows dejection and giving up. In the meantime Minnie has moved in closer to Sharon and is standing quietly.

"Is this the first time you have told him this?"

"No, I guess not. I have told him a couple of times but he does not seem to listen."

"What do you do when he doesn't listen?"

"Nothing, I guess."

I stepped out of the way.

"Sharon, I want you to lunge Minnie again, but this time I want you to imagine she is your boyfriend and as you lunge her, tell her how you feel about not listening to you, and your situation."

Sharon lunges Minnie again, this time getting her to go around the circle a couple of times.

"Now tell her what you are going to do if you cannot come out in the open about your relationship."

Sharon snaps the whip and with tears in her eyes tells Minnie that she will end the relationship unless they can come out in the open.

Minnie trots a few steps and stops. I encourage Sharon again and once, twice more she attempts to get Minnie going and keep her trotting the circle until she asks her to stop. Minnie continues to trot a few steps, turn and look at Sharon and stop.

Knowing we were at an impasse for the day, I end the session.

Sharon was not able to follow through with getting Minnie to trot until she was given the command to stop. It was obvious to both of us that she was not ready to follow through with her threat of ending the relationship with her boyfriend.

INSIGHTS:

Follow-through is essential to be a successful leader of self and others. When we do not follow through with what we say we will do we first lose self- respect and then others lose respect for us. Without respect there will be no follow-ship. By practicing self- honesty we know what we want and what we are willing to do to get there. Therefore we do not set ourselves up to give empty ultimatums.

To be a successful leader who inspires follow-ship implies that we have love and respect from those we lead. To inspire love and respect from others you must first love yourself enough to demand this respectful treatment. You will be treated as you expect to be treated.

⁓ Deepen your Partnership

Bell's red roan hair coat looks almost white from the distance where she is peacefully grazing out in the pasture. She raises her head, momentarily ceasing to eat, and looks over at me standing by the fence. Even from our twenty-foot distance I can see her quiet, sensitive eyes. Perceptive, she can read me and always knows what is going on below my polite or political face.

Staring into her eyes I can feel the thread of emotion that passes between us. We are able to read each other at a subconscious level, making our connection to each other especially strong. Our deep connection developed slowly over time almost without my even realizing it was happening.

I bought her as a two-year-old and she came a little wild and pushy. She had never been handled much. Therefore it took some time to teach her ground manners and respect like not walking over the top of me when I led her and no pushing over the top of me to get into the barn at night. Now that she is six we have spent the time together to build our relationship and trust. She knows that I am going to take care of her and while she respects me she has no fear of me. We have grown to love and trust each other.

On several occasions I have attempted to get her ready to be a show horse and though she has the breeding and the looks it has never worked out. Each time we were close it came down to the fact that she would need to be forced into a role that did not fit for her so each time I backed off.

Like Minnie they were destined to be mothers and brood mares and they love their job. Finally realizing and accepting Bell's natural abilities I have allowed her to be who she is without forcing her into a role that did not fit her natural talents or her desires. She is beautiful to look at, very striking and different with her roan hair coat like Dolly Parton's coat of many colors so she draws a lot of attention wherever she goes. She stands in people terms a little over five feet and weighs around a thousand pounds. Not a huge mare but a substantial one with hocks that sit up under her and drive deep and soft just the way you want them to.

I have noticed that with horses, as with people, there are those that you can connect with at a deeper level than others and Bell and I have that emotional connection. She would do anything she could for me and I for her.

Over time as I have led her around I have naturally, without conscious thought, put my right hand on the right side of her face with me walking to her left side. As time has progressed I have found that she allows me to lead her without a halter just by having my fingertips on her cheek. When she was hurt this was the only way we could lead her into the trailer since her face was cut open. To lead in this way takes an enormous amount of trust and respect on both our parts. It's something we do without conscious thought. If she chose she could barrel right over the top of me and hurt me very badly. She has all the physical power over me. Having gained her trust and respect she gives me the emotional power.

This is a huge responsibility. With this emotional power I could do much damage to her. This gift she has given me is an honor and a responsibility that I never take lightly.

INSIGHTS:

Real Power comes from connecting on an emotional level. Bell had the physical power but gave me the emotional power because over time we had developed a bond of trust and respect. When you take the time to build trust and respect and to connect at a deep emotional level you have achieved leadership and relationship on a higher plane. Leadership at this level has more impact and elicits greater allegiance. When a person allows you to connect on this emotional level they have bestowed on you an honor and also a responsibility. You have a new power with them that is not to be taken lightly. Great leaders know the benefit of this emotional connection.

Leadership
is walking alongside,
guiding beyond
the fear.

⌒ Walk Alongside

Sylk is frantically running from one end of the pasture to the other. She is in a total panic and her body is soaking wet with nervous sweat. I can hear her screaming even though I am inside the house with all the doors and windows shut. All this because we have the irrigation sprinklers on to water the pasture. Our ranch is located east of the mountains about two hours from Seattle. The land here needs to be irrigated to get grass to grow and today is our irrigation day. Sylk, my six-year-old mare, is irrationally afraid of the irrigation pipes. Even though she gets frequent baths to get her ready to compete at the horseshows, for her there is something very different about the water coming up from the pipes on the ground. Hence our problem.

The water sprays out from the irrigation pipes that are lying across the pasture lengthwise twenty or thirty feet apart. The water makes a hissing and spurting sound as it jets up and then over the pastures. We have five rows of pipes in each pasture with the horse barn sitting in between the pastures. They can hear and see the water as it sprays up from the pipes. When it is our schedule to water the pastures they run twenty-four hours a day for four days in a row. To take Sylk on a trail ride I will pass not only our irrigation pipes but several neighbors' as well. Therefore it is important to get her quiet and calm around the water as it sprays onto the pastures. Cliff and I discussed how to get her feeling easy with them and decided to put her out in the pasture with the pipes for several hours a day. In this way we expect her to become adapted to them and get over her fear, a fear which sends her into a running frenzy.

As planned, this afternoon Cliff is headed out to take her to the pasture where the sprinkler system is on. What I had in mind was to put her in the pasture, let her go, and then leave her there for a while. Cliff took her out to the pasture, which is about the size of a small baseball field, and proceeded to walk her back and forth across the pasture. Sylk was so afraid that most of the walking was done with her running sideways up and down getting ever closer to the water. Sylk kept jumping and running sideways as Cliff inched her closer to the jet streams of water. Each time she jumped he would stop and pet her neck with a slow soothing slide of his hand down her neck to her shoulder. I was watching him from the window and could see him as he talked quietly to her. He walked her up one side of the field then back down the other side and pretty soon he had them both in the spray from the water.

Imagine my surprise when Sylk lifted her head up and opened her mouth to let the water flow into her mouth, taking a nice long drink. Cliff was dripping wet from head to toe and I thought he would stop now that Sylk had taken her drink of water but, being the patient and persistent person that he is, he just kept leading her up and down the pasture until he was sure that she was comfortable. So now some forty-five minutes later he unsnaps her halter and turns her free in the pasture.

INSIGHTS:

Leadership is walking alongside. Our fears can look irrational to the outside observer and a successful leader will have many responsibilities and be very busy fulfilling those responsibilities. So when a person demonstrates what to them may seem like an irrational fear, the initial reaction may be to send them out on their own with some instruction on how to overcome their fear. First it is important to note that regardless of how inconsequential the fears may seem to others, for the person who has the fears they may be huge and can keep them from reaching their goals and objectives. If you feel it then it is valid and it does not matter if anyone else feels it. A wise leader will walk alongside leading through the fear and discomfort. When you lead individuals through their fears, they will be more successful in overcoming their fears and excelling in their roles.

Leaders will do well to pay attention to the actions of the individual. If a person is consistently not meeting his goals and hanging back, he may have some hidden fears that need to be addressed. An effective leader knows that merely telling people not to be afraid is not an effective solution for reducing, or helping them overcome, their fears.

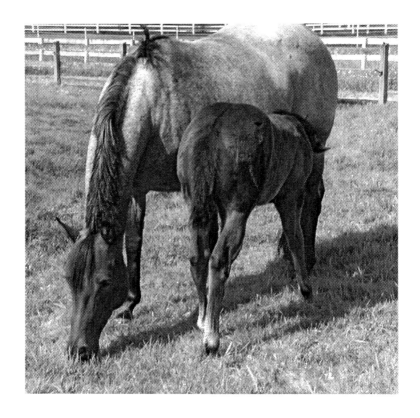

Karma and Tasha as a foal

⌒ Take Your Spurs Off

Tasha has spur marks on both sides of her stomach and the hair is rubbed off down to the skin. Her skin is an irritated pink color and looks raw and sore, like a blister from wearing new shoes that slide up and down on your heel might. When I go to touch her sides she moves away from me, afraid of my touch.

Tasha is tall and elegant, a deep bay brown color with quiet, expressive eyes. Her breeding is of top bloodlines because we bred her to be a top western pleasure contender. She has been the envy of trainers since she was just a year old and we all assumed she was going to be one of the best. As a breeder this is what you breed for: excellent bloodlines, quiet, beautiful, and talented. After we get them started under saddle I always send my young horses out to a trainer to further their education and training in preparation for their show career. So as usual I have Tasha boarded out with Linda for training. But as we move towards our goal something is wrong and it is causing me to lose sleep at night.

Closing my eyes I can see Tasha's elegant body and big expressive eyes questioning and accusing me.

"I thought you loved me."

"I thought I could trust you."

"Why have you sent me away? "

"I am trying, why won't you accept me for who I am?"

"Why are you trying to get me to do something I cannot do?"

"Is something wrong with me?"

"Do you want me to be someone else?"

Tasha's eyes bore into my soul and I know that there will be no relief until I confront the issue and get it resolved.

The next morning with Tasha by my side I tell Linda to slow her training down. After we spend some time talking we decide that Tasha is not ready for the rigors of western pleasure training just yet and may need to wait a few months.

"But you know she will not be ready for the fall futurities, right?" Linda questions me.

Turning my face and eyes to the sky I think about this for a minute. As a breeder it is hard to let go of the goal to enter her into the competition where she will advertise my breeding program. My stomach tightens as I realize it is my pride and ego that are standing in the way, but even recognizing that my selfish ego wants to control, I still find it hard to let go of my goals. But I know that I need to do what is best for Tasha regardless of my personal goals. In the end she has to be number one.

I swallow hard struggling to let go of my goals.

"I know she won't but that is the way it has to be."

INSIGHTS:

> Trust is built on a solid foundation. One of the methods that will build a solid foundation is your willingness to let go of your personal goals when required to care for the needs of others. Building follow-ship will only happen in a spirit of trust.

Successful leaders will sacrifice their goals for the greater good.

Effective leaders look for and lead to a person's natural talents and abilities where they can encourage rather than force. When individuals operate with their strengths and abilities, rather than being forced into a role that intensifies their weaknesses, their chances for successful performance increases ten-fold.

We gave Tasha some time to grow up and just rode her lightly throughout the summer. When we thought she was more ready we started her training again with some new methods. Now a year later she is ready to be shown on the pleasure circuit and will be the top contender she was bred to be. A beautiful mover we have high hopes for her this year. But it could have been a different scenario altogether if we had pushed her into a role that did not fit at that time in her life. The role of a leader is always to act in the best interest of the individuals we lead.

Bell and Jean

Give Them Freedom to Roam

Bell, my most treasured brood mare, is a beautiful red roan color. She has black legs and her face, while predominately black, has a nice white blaze down the front and her body has various shades of red, black, and white colors. She stands out from the crowd with her beauty and is exceptionally quiet and easy to be around. She has the ability to look deep within your soul with her big soft eyes. I bought her as a two-year- old and immediately fell in love with her. Her main job is having beautiful and talented babies.

We have moved to the east side of the mountains and it has started to rain. Being accustomed to the continual rain and mud on the west side of the mountains we make a quick decision to put up some temporary shelter for the horses since we have not yet had the time to finish the barn. We want the mares to at least have a dry place to sleep for the night.

This morning Cliff goes out to feed but immediately runs back into the house to get me. As soon as I see his face I know that something is wrong.

"Bell is hurt" he yells as he comes in the door.

"We need to get a veterinarian right away."

Feeling a little panicky I grab my coat on my way out the door and race out to the barn. My stomach tightens and I swallow hard trying not to be sick. Bell is standing looking at me with so much pain in her eyes that I can hardly bear to look at her. Her cheekbone is sliced open, hanging and dripping blood. On further inspection I see that her front leg is also ripped open behind the knee so badly she can hardly walk and blood is dripping from it as well. Now feeling total panic I know that we have to get her some medical help right away. Being new in town we had not yet established ourselves with a veterinarian so running back into the house I scan the yellow pages and beginning from the top start phoning to see who I can get out. To make matters worse, today is Saturday so many of the offices are closed. After several phone calls I finally find a clinic that is open and they can see her but only if we can trailer her into them. Having no idea how we are going to load her into the trailer since her face is cut so badly it is impossible to put a halter on her, I tell them we will be there soon, and head out the door.

While I croon soothingly to Bell Cliff gets the trailer hooked up and ready to go. I have been mulling over how we will get Bell in the trailer so I have him put Sylk in the trailer first. Bell will have more incentive to load with another horse in the trailer. Cliff hands me a lead rope and I lay it over Bell's neck being careful not to touch her face. Lucky for us I had made it a habit to lead Bell in and out of the pasture by lightly holding the off side of her face even though she had a halter on. This turns out to be our saving grace. I gently put my hand on the other side of her face and lead her to the trailer in this way. She walked with me beside her into the trailer without blinking an eye.

We know and love each other and I am sure this is the only way I am able to get her into the trailer with nothing more than my hand on her cheek. We get her to the vet and get her face and leg stitched and bandaged. We will have several weeks of daily cleaning and bandaging in order to help her recover but at least she will be all right.

Driving to the vet we finally have the time to figure out as best we can what had happened. We are feeling pretty bad since we know that it was our decision to put Bell in the pen and had we not made that decision she would not be hurt. The gate that we had used had a sharp edge on it that we had inadvertently missed last night in our hurry to get a shelter up for them. Bell must have spooked at something during the night and tried to get out of the pen. Most likely when she could not get out she panicked even more and hurt herself.

We knew that we had made our decision with the horses' best interests in mind. We were attempting to protect them from the weather. Even with their best interest in mind, we had made a wrong decision for Bell. In trying to protect her we had put her in harm's way.

INSIGHTS:

Leaders, though you may think the best strategy is to protect your followers, this is not always possible or even advisable. You will want to examine each episode to make a conscious decision on whether protection is right in any given situation. In general we want to guide rather than try to protect. In many situations walking through the dilemma is what teaches us and those we lead. We learn by doing, not by being told what to do. Effective leaders give themselves a break and know that even though they make the best decisions they can, sometimes these decisions lead to pain for others. Forgive yourself.

By spending the time and energy up front to build a trusting and respectful relationship with your teams you will find that in times of stress and uncertainty they will instinctively trust and follow you. This seemingly simple thing can make the difference in reaching your goals or falling short. These instinctive reactions will make a major difference in your ability to lead on a day-to-day basis in many ways that you will not even be aware of until the episode happens. Instinctive follow-ship is critical to your success as a leader.

⌒ SHARE YOURSELF

Karma, with her big doe eyes, is standing quietly in the corner of the arena as Jo and I walk in. She is a big, stout blue roan mare who stands in people terms about six feet tall. She has a broad back and can easily carry a two hundred-plus-pound man or woman and not look under-sized. Karma has big, soft brown eyes and while a big, stout mare, she is also an exceptionally quiet mare. She was the leader of the herd for years but something happened between them and lately her sister Bell has taken over the lead mare role in the herd. She is a kind mare who likes to show love and have love shown to her. She is the one I seek out when I have had a bad day and put my arms around her neck and tell her all about my day. I always feel better afterwards like she has heard me and really cares.

Jo has leadership responsibilities and she has come today because she finds herself near tears much of the time. Her lack of patience with those at work is causing her problems in her position. Her body is physically telling her to slow down but rather than listening and making changes she snaps at people at work and at her family for little things. She has told me she feels like she is near a breaking point and needs help.

In our conversations I have learned that Jo is the oldest child from an alcoholic marriage. Her pattern in life has been to take on other people's issues and try to rescue them.

She has a very bubbly personality and likes to cut up and have a good time with people. But she keeps her fears and hurts hidden inside. She feels she is losing control of her life both at home and at work.

Karma has just the right quiet and loving spirit but she can also be a strong mare when she needs to be. This makes me think she is the perfect horse to work with Jo today. Putting on "The Piano Magic of Floyd Cramer" and allowing the music to drift around us, I walk with Jo into the center of the arena and leave Karma free to roam around as she wants to. The first exercise we will do is to get Jo to slow down, get quiet, and center herself. Talking Jo through each step, I ask her to focus on each area of her body. I want her to listen to what her body is telling her. If there are areas of tension in her body that need release then we will find them as we take time to listen to each area. We work down from her head and shoulders and I sense the tension in her shoulders. My stomach starts to tighten and I sense that Jo is also holding tension and fear in her stomach. When we have completed the centering exercise I decide to put Jo in close contact with Karma.

"Jo, I want you to walk with Karma, touch her, caress her, and just spend time with her."

"I am going to stand back so you have total privacy with her. You can tell her anything. Tell her some of the difficulties you are facing and how you feel about them."

"All right," Jo responds as she walks towards Karma.

Karma had walked in close to us while we were doing the centering exercise and had waited patiently for us to finish.

Walking to the end of the arena I leave the music playing softly so that Jo has privacy in her time with Karma. Jo spends a few minutes talking to Karma and breaks down crying. I am hoping she will spend time with her and really let go but she lets her guard down for only a short time and then quickly composes herself again. Not willing to show her vulnerability, she turns and looks at me.

When I see she is finished I walk over to them. Karma has been standing quietly as if she senses the pain and stress that Jo is holding inside. She seems to be saying she is willing to take Jo's pain on herself. When Jo walks over to me Karma walks over with her and stands beside her. It is clear that she wants to be with Jo.

"Jo, did you tell Karma what is going on for you today?"

"Yes, I did, at least a little."

"What did you feel in your time with Karma?

"Well I felt like she was listening to me and that she cared."

"Anything else?

Taking a deep breath Jo answers, "I felt like she was willing to take my problems on her shoulders."

"Are you willing to allow her to?"

Jo laughs nervously. "No, I am not willing to do that."

Jo's shoulders are tight and stiff as she continues. "I can't do that. I can't put my stuff on her. They are my problems."

I am clearer now about what is happening for Jo at work as we talk through this exercise. "What does it mean to you to be a leader?"

Tipping her head to the side quizzically, she says," I'm not sure what you mean."

"Are you taking on all the responsibilities and problems, thinking you need to take care of them all?"

"I'm not sure, maybe I do."

"Tell me about the last time you had a big project due at work. Who did the planning, organizing, and follow-up?"

Jo swallows hard and clearly is attempting to remember if she allowed her reports to do their jobs or if she had taken over the whole project. With a long sigh she finally responds, "If I don't do it then I am afraid it won't get done and it is my job that is at stake."

"Let's look at what happened with Karma. Didn't you agree that Karma was willing to take on some of the burdens you feel?"

"Yes, but I cannot put them on Karma."

"But you told me that you are nearing a breaking point. That you have too much to do and can't get it done and you are emotionally exhausted."

"Yes, but if I do not do it then it won't get done," Jo insists once again.

"But do you see that by taking on all the burdens that you do not allow others to help you nor to grow themselves?"

"Is it lack of trust of others or lack of trust in yourself that causes you to keep things to yourself?"

Jo is unable to answer the questions that I am asking her. Since we have accomplished our goal for the day, which was to help Jo become aware of her self-defeating patterns in her leadership role, we finish the day with an assignment for the week.

"Jo, I would like for you to spend some time this week thinking about why it is difficult for you to let go of control. What are you afraid of when you let go of control? What would really happen if you did let go of control?"

Insights:

Inspiring follow-ship, by its very nature means that you are sharing yourself with others. When you the leader close off from those you lead because of your own fears you shut down your emotional connection. By not allowing your followers to share in who you are, you make a trusting relationship impossible. They will know when as their leader you feel it necessary to maintain control. But rather than assume it is about your fears they assume it is because you do not have trust in them and their abilities. When a leader insists on keeping the control and not allowing others to take on their own responsibilities they break the leadership foundations of trust, connection, and mutual respect. Without a firm foundation it will be impossible to be successful in your leadership role. Leadership is guiding those you lead through their own successes and failures rather than simply taking on the work yourself. A great leader allows for mistakes and provides the safety nets while allowing learning through doing. Only by riding the horse does one learn to ride the horse, not by the telling how to ride.

Snickers

CHAPTER 5

Taking the Reins with Feel

⟿ SETTING DIRECTION AND LEADING toward GOALS

Performing your leadership role with Feel is to be in such total harmony with the persons you lead that you flow and move toward your goals as if you were one. Taking the reins with Feel takes time but provides the leader with a solid foundation on which to build.

*Authenticity
is acting on the outside
who you are
on the inside.*

⌒ Show Up and Stay in the Present

Minnie is standing in the middle of the arena waiting to see what we want. Her ears are forward as she watches us. She is extremely sensitive to her environment and those in it and right now she is feeling nervous because she does not know what to do with herself. She is tall, regal, and coal-black, with the most beautiful head and expressive eyes I have ever seen. When being defiant her eyes turn hard as steel. If she is nervous or afraid her eyes go wide and the white shows all around her eyeballs, making her look a little like a cat ready to spring at the slightest hint of danger.

Beverly is here for a coaching session. After talking about safety issues we get started. Beverly is a manager in a local software company and is having some issues with her reports; our goal today is to help her uncover the problems. I put some soft melodic music on as we get started in our session. The rhythm is soft and relaxing and sets the stage for our work.

"Beverly, please turn with your back to Minnie and close your eyes while I take you through this exercise."

"You do not need to be afraid or worry about Minnie because I will watch her and keep you safe should she decide to come too close to you."

As we proceed with the exercise my intuition kicks in and I know that Beverly is tense in her back and seems to be carrying stress throughout her body. Though her body is quiet her mind is active and confused and she has a hard time allowing herself to focus. My goal is to slow the process of life down for her long enough so she can tune into her body and what it is telling her. Her body has the answers she seeks if she can just hear it speaking. We spend time talking about the stress she is holding and what might be the causes. We may not solve the reasons for her stress today but becoming aware of them is the first step in the process.

Next I ask Beverly to move Minnie around the arena in whatever way works best for her. I give her a few tips on how she might go about the assignment.

"I can't get her to go."

"Why won't she trot around like I am asking her to do?

"She is just looking at me and not moving."

Beverly is getting more and more agitated and Minnie is lazily wandering around, coming in close to Beverly, looking at her with a question in her eyes and then lazily walking off again. I allow this to continue for five minutes or so before I intervene. I am hoping that Beverly will begin to see what is happening but she is getting more and more confused. Her energy level is extremely low and instead of raising it up and moving Minnie around she begins to caress her shoulder. Minnie stands quiet beside her and it is clear that she is aware that what Beverly needs right now is just quiet affection.

"Beverly, let's look at what just happened for you."

"Clearly Minnie was waiting for you to tell her what to do."

"She kept coming back to you over and over again waiting for you to tell her and show her what you wanted."

"Instead you acted like you were asking her but then you stopped short of really asking her what you wanted of her."

"She wanted direction, and you gave her none. So she was confused and finally just stood still."

"Now what is happening with your employees at work?"

"Are they doing the same thing?"

With a look of surprise on her face, Beverly answered, "Yes, they are."

"Now tell me what your problem really is. I don't think it is with your employees. I think it lies with you."

Beverly started to cry and we spent the next few minutes talking about the problems she was facing with her children and her lack of direction in her life.

She was unhappy in her management role and at the same time her adult children were at a crossroads in their lives, which was taking her emotional energy. She did not have an answer for either situation and having them both come at the same time was leaving her drained and depressed. She was in operation overload and had simply shut down in order to cope, leaving her employees "alone" even though she was physically there.

While we were talking Minnie walked over to the compact disc player, bumped into it and stopped the music I was playing. She somehow switched it to Vince Gill's smooth melody singing about calling him and he will be there for you, telling us that it is ok to let our tears fall down like rain, that tomorrow the sun will shine all we have to do is take it one day at a time. The song and the music were perfect and left us with no doubt that "someone" was guiding the process.

Minnie and the universe knew that Beverly needed rest, love, and time to reenergize and had acted to give her what she needed today.

Insights:

To inspire follow-ship you have to show up, be there, and be available to those you lead; not only in body but in mind and spirit. You may think you are hiding your emotional withdrawal but indeed your lack of emotional connection and being plugged into your group is highly visible and disturbing. When you the leader withdraw you leave those who would follow you hanging. Without clear direction they will first ask in a variety of ways, then still not getting the leadership direction from you, they will come to a standstill. After a time they may begin to circle the wagons so to speak and begin making an effort to move. But their movements will be confused, slow, and have a lack of full purpose and direction.

Being available in body only leaves your followers feeling futile and can elicit anger and leadership position overthrow, back-stabbing behaviors, and unhappiness. True leadership is much more than a role; when you leave the connection you could find that you have the role position for a time but without the real follow-ship that is needed for your success.

An effective leader must be clear and focused in order to impart focus and direction to those they lead.

⌒ CREATE PHYSICAL MEMORY

The sun is blazing orange overhead but the lack of humidity along with a slight breeze makes it not only bearable but comfortable here in eastern Washington. The warmth with the sun shining down on her makes Sylk docile and a little lethargic. We have a horse show later this month where she will compete in a western pleasure class so we are training to get ready for it. Sylk and I have already had our time in the round pen. She is ready for our riding session.

Climbing into the saddle I begin our ride by tapping both heels against Sylk's sides to get her into a walk. Clucking to her I ask her to trot around the perimeter of the arena. The arena is eighty feet long by one-hundred-thirty feet wide, which gives us plenty of room to work on the arena wall and inside the center. Trotting her down the length of the arena I pull her off the rail several times, turning her into the center and making a small circle and then back onto the wall again. After we warm up with this exercise we are ready to progress to the next step.

First I want her to trot staying on the rail wall of the arena just as we will in the show pen on a loose rein. She needs to go around at a consistent slow jog trot with her shoulders elevated and her hocks driving deep and slow up under her. When we ask our horses to trot slow and deep it is hard for them and more work to keep their shoulders up and have self-carriage. Sylk has a tendency to want to drop her shoulders down and move more on her front end, which keeps her from driving as deep and strong as she should with her hocks.

Giving her a little more rein and guiding her to the side of the arena I use my inside leg to hold her slightly in place. We begin our jog around the arena. I want to give her the chance to trot around correctly with no interference on my part. We trot about three-quarters of the way around the arena with Sylk keeping her shoulders up and driving deep and slow with her hocks.

Then Sylk begins to get a little lazy and drops her shoulders, which causes her to trot sloppy with her weight on the front end of her body. Pressing my legs into her sides I lift my hands just slightly. I am hoping that the lift on the reins and my legs will get Sylk to lift her shoulders up again. She lifts her head up but leaves her shoulders down.

Next I guide her off the rail and into the center of the arena where I have six bright orange cones set up about three feet apart in a straight line. Using my legs to apply pressure to her left side and then to her right side I jog her around one cone after the other, putting her in the position of jogging a serpentine pattern around the cones. By jogging the serpentine Sylk has a hard time dropping her shoulders; each turn is followed by another and then another. This makes it almost impossible for her to drop her shoulders since she is always turning and must use her front legs and shoulders to make the turns. In this exercise I make dropping her shoulders hard and keeping them up easy for her to do. This teaches her body to stay in the correct position without my continually correcting her.

After spending ten minutes jogging the serpentine we are able to resume our place on the rail. This time Sylk holds her shoulders up several laps around the arena before once again she gets lazy and starts to drop her shoulders down once more.

As soon as I feel her dropping her shoulders down I propel her back into the center of the arena and into the serpentine exercise. We spend ten more minutes in the center jogging the serpentine. This time when I jog her back out to the rail her body remembers the correct position and we complete our ride on the rail without interruption. She keeps her shoulders up and drives deep.

INSIGHTS:

Tell them, they know it for a day; teach them, they know it for lifetime. Most anyone can tell someone else what to do but great leadership is being resourceful enough to guide individuals by allowing them to find the way themselves. When we are told how to do something we know it for a day but when we learn how to do something by doing it successfully ourselves we internalize it and the knowledge becomes a part of us. Great leaders are great teachers. People must learn for themselves to really know it, whatever it may be. So the first thing we must do as great leaders is to give others the chance to do it right before we give correction. While giving proper instruction is important to their success, after giving the instructions we need to allow people the opportunity to perform the action themselves. Rather than giving them correction, an inventive leader will set their followers up for success by making the right thing easy and the wrong thing hard. This allows the person an opportunity to find the correct path without overt interference from the leader. Learning in this way is much more satisfying and much more memorable. On the opposite scale, continually correcting is irritating and self-defeating.

It is important for an effective leader to know that our bodies have memory cells. What we learn with the mind and body is remembered longer and better. An effective leader will set up opportunities for their team members to learn at a mind and body level. Once the body has the knowledge and ability to complete an activity then it will do this activity robotically without needing to consciously think about it. This can be very advantageous to a leader and their teams in their efforts to reach their goals.

⁓ Manage the Fight or Flight Response

Halle is standing on the far side of the round pen. Her eyes are wide and her stance is stiff and tense. She is our two-year-old black quarter horse mare. All her instincts are on red alert so when Cliff walks over to her to caress her shoulders she jumps away automatically without thinking. A tall black mare with normally nice, big, quiet eyes, she is a little butt high right now because she is going through a growing spurt. She is not sure what is coming but she is sure she would rather be out in the pasture at play or eating.

Cliff has rigged up a big black plastic garbage bag that he has tied to the end of a lunge whip and while he is not doing anything with it yet, Halle senses something is coming. He also has a big blue plastic tarp lying in the pen. There is a slight breeze today so the plastic is moving and making some crackling noises. When faced with something that is new to them and especially something that is making a noise and not knowing what it is, a horse will instinctively want to run from it. They have a fight or flight survival mode of operation so if they cannot get away from something that frightens them then they will try to paw at it with their front feet. Their first instinctive reaction, though, is to run, which is why when working with them, you want to give them an escape door (so to speak) rather than closing all avenues for escape. Knowing this, Cliff is allowing Halle the freedom of the round pen for these first few minutes so she can become somewhat less fearful of the new sounds and sights of the plastic.

Cliff sits down on the blue mounting block in the round pen and stays quiet for a few minutes allowing Halle time to de-stress. He gives her about five minutes just to be in the pen with the new objects, then he picks up the whip with the black plastic bag tied to it and begins moving it left and right, causing it to make a swishing sound as it glides through the air. Hearing the noise Halle begins to run around the pen a little wildly. Cliff acts like nothing is happening and stays seated on the blue mounting block and simply continues to wave the whip with the black plastic bag in the air. After running around for a few minutes and seeing that nothing is coming after her, Halle stops and stares at the black plastic bag. When she stops and looks at it, Cliff stops the movement of the bag and puts it up under her nose so she can smell it. With a small breeze still blowing, the black plastic moves a little in the breeze so that it blows in Halle's face. She jumps back from the black bag, but Cliff follows her with it and pretty soon she stands quiet with the bag up next to her face.

Cliff swishes the black plastic bag back and forth behind her hindquarters. Feeling the pressure of the bag and the noise Halle takes off into a gallop around the pen. Cliff just keeps swishing the plastic bag behind her and again after a few more minutes of galloping around the pen and seeing that nothing is hurting her, Halle slows down and even though the black plastic bag is still at her hindquarters, she begins to listen to Cliff as he talks to her, giving her commands of jog, then walk, and then whoa.

Next Cliff spends a good half an hour or more repeating the movements and allowing Halle to get more and more comfortable with the plastic bag. When she is comfortable with the black plastic bag behind her, he hooks it to the side of the round pen and asks her to jog around the pen and go past the plastic blowing in the breeze. At first she veers to the inside of the pen while attempting to stay clear of the bag, but as he continues to push her closer and closer to the wall with his body, she eventually jogs right through the plastic bag with it hitting her on the shoulder.

Lastly he drags the blue plastic tarp into her path on the perimeter of the round pen so that she has to walk over it to get around the pen. At first she tries to go around the tarp but again he pushes her out with his body and she has nowhere to go but over the top of the tarp. Once or twice she attempts to jump the blue tarp but sees this is futile; after all it did not hurt her so finally she just walks over the top of it. Indeed after a while she acts like she has always jogged over a blue tarp and of course it is no big deal.

To finish, Cliff picks up the blue tarp and lays it over her back sliding it off and then putting it back on several times. Then he leaves it on her back and asks her to walk off. Halle walks off with the blue tarp on her back, sliding and swishing around till it finally falls, at which point she just walks over the top of it.

INSIGHTS:

Feeling the fear is not as important as what you do when you feel the fear. Have you ever wondered where you might be in your life today on a personal or professional level if you had adopted the feel-the-fear-and-do-it-anyway attitude and actions? What if you never allowed fear to stand in your way? Fear comes in all shapes and sizes, fear of failure, fear of success, fear of looking silly, fear of not having enough, and numerous other fears our mind creates. The more you fear and do not move through the fear the more frozen with fear you become. With our horses we take a step-by-step approach to helping them overcome their fears. We don't start out by throwing plastic over the top of their head any more than you might start out doing a speech in front of a thousand-person audience. We start by allowing them to see, smell, and touch the plastic and then by shaking it in front of them and finally by throwing it over their backs. You might start out with a speech in front of a fifty-person chamber of commerce and then a two hundred-person association and then finally the thousand-person audience. A wise leader of self and others develops a strategy of overcoming what looks like an insurmountable fear by leading them through the fear with a step-by-step strategy until our followers have accomplished climbing the mountain when at first they were afraid to climb a hill.

⌒ Expect 100%

I am working with Joe, a four-year-old bay gelding in the round pen. He does not really want to work. He is a little on the lazy side and would much rather come into the center of the pen with me. He keeps trying to stop and turn into me as an escape. He acts like he is being submissive so that he can stop but when I actually ask him to listen to my commands he rebels, either by turning into me, stopping, or running around in the pen. I clearly do not have his attention or his respect.

Spending the next thirty minutes with him, I get him to trot around the pen a few strides and then turn him to go the other direction. We do this over and over again until he begins to listen to my requests. Then I work with him on whoa when I ask him to rather than waiting four feet after I have requested it. Don, his owner, has told me that he has been advised by his trainer that Joe needs a better work ethic. This is the first time I have worked with Joe so I don't want to push him too much the first day. After we accomplish gaining his attention and respect for the day, I quit.

Now it is Don's turn in the round pen with Joe. I want to see how Joe interacts with Don and what they are able to get accomplished. Don asks Joe to walk around the pen, then turn and walk the other way. Joe walks and trots around the pen with Don turning him a few times. Initially Joe is on the outside perimeter of the pen as Don asks him to walk and trot. Gradually, as Don is working with Joe, Joe begins to move off the perimeter of the round pen and ease his way into the pen, making his walk- or trot-around shorter and shorter. In this way he has less distance to cover.

"Don, Joe is cheating you by moving into the pen so he does not have to work as hard."

"Push him out to the perimeter of the pen, by using the whip as an extension of your arm and walking towards him."

"Okay," Don answers as he walks towards Joe.

Don walks towards Joe but falls short of getting him to move over to the outside of the pen. Joe moves a few steps but quickly comes back off the wall of the pen as he trots around. Again I ask Don to push him out to the wall and again he moves him over some but then watches as Joe moves back into the pen and does nothing to push him back out.

"Don, do you realize that Joe is cheating you by cutting into the round pen?"

"Well, yes, I guess so."

"By allowing him to come into the round pen instead of staying out on the wall, you are telling him that you are satisfied with halfway. So he can give you halfway and you will be satisfied with that."

With a little laugh, Don says, "I guess that is what I do with my kids and people I lead as well."

"Yes, that is probably true," I respond as we end our work.

INSIGHTS:

Inspiring follow-ship is always about expecting our teams to give their all. Giving their all means they give to the best of their ability. As leaders it is our job to challenge our followers and never allow them to cheat themselves or us by giving halfway effort. You will find that some followers have a natural inclination to attempt to cut corners. This is simply a personality trait that needs to be managed like any other. It is also, for some, a natural personality trait to push against the leadership boundaries to see what their leader will accept. To achieve the desired results, practice appropriate firmness. As an effective leader we are never satisfied with halfway effort or work. Instead we ask for and expect the best from those we lead and are never satisfied until they give us their best.

Likewise in our leadership of self we are never satisfied with halfway attempts of success. We adopt the adage of keeping on until we are achieving our best, never allowing for halfway effort.

Halle and Cliff

⌒ Vet Your Destination Before Your Ride

Eve is working with a big-bodied, tall sorrel gelding called Jim. Her assignment is to ask him to move his hindquarters around by applying pressure with her right palm while turning his head towards his right shoulder with her left hand. While this is not a difficult exercise it is one that requires focus and concentration. I have several other people in the arena working on the same exercise so I give them instructions and then step back to observe them in action.

I watch as Eve attempts to calm Jim down so she can complete the exercise. Jim, a normally quiet and easy-going gelding, is bouncing around and paying no attention to Eve's pleas to whoa. I notice that Eve seems be full of energy; you know the kind of energy that you see in children sometimes where they just do not know what to do with themselves. She keeps moving the horse around, trying to get him to focus and he keeps trying to walk off, then jog around her, paying no attention whatsoever to her commands. No matter what Eve does, Jim only seems to get more agitated, upset, and confused. Eve is getting very frustrated and so is Jim. While Eve seems from the outside view to be giving the right cues to Jim, she is clearly not succeeding in getting what she wants him to do. I am quite fascinated and keep watching to see what is going to happen. Horses are a mirror image of what is going on with the person; I know that even though Eve seems to be giving the right cues, something is indeed very wrong with their interaction.

Moving in closer I can sense Eve's high energy and stress. Her emotional energy feels so tense that it makes me uncomfortable just to be close to her. I was beginning to feel sorry for Jim. While her body was here exhibiting high stressful energy, her mind was seemingly on many other things and her frustration is bubbling over the top. Though she seems to be asking Jim to turn his head and move his hip over, she does not act like she really expects him to complete the exercise. It feels more like she is giving lip service to the request. A few more minutes of this and I know that she is not going to accomplish her task without help.

I motion for Cliff to come in to her. Walking over he calmly takes Jim's lead and asks him to turn his head and move his hindquarters over. Jim settles down immediately and does as he is asked. I want Eve to understand what has happened on her own with no interference on my part so I wait to see how she will respond.

She stands perfectly still for a minute with a look on her face that has to be one of those "aha" moments and I can see her take several deep breaths. It's clear to me that she has now balanced herself and become focused. She is now clear in her mind, not only what in she wants from her horse but in exactly how to ask him for it. Then, in one beautiful, purposeful step, she asks and he obliges, gracefully and flawlessly.

INSIGHTS:

High energy with no clear intention brings chaos to any situation and to the people in that situation. Leadership requires focused, consistent energy with a purpose. High energy with activity for activity's sake rarely accomplishes your goals. You must first know exactly what you want to happen before you ask those you lead for activity. Your purpose must be clear and your communication needs to be specific so that the person knows exactly what you are asking for. Ask with the expectation of getting what you ask for.

Jean and Halle

⌒ Find Alternative Trails

My two-year-old filly Dee is anxiously stomping her feet. Her red sorrel hair coat looks bright in the foggy morning air. Her eyes, big and expressive, show her worry. Looking at me and then out to the arena she is feeling the stress of being out of her comfort zone.

Our work area is one-hundred feet wide by two-hundred long and right now has mud puddles that cover the full length and width with only a few dry spots where the ground is a little higher. Dee knows this is not going to be fun today. I can almost hear her audibly moan,

"I just want to go back inside to my nice warm stall."

"My hay is waiting for me and it is nice and dry inside so after I eat I can take a nap."

"I don't know what she wants of me today but it sure doesn't look like fun."

It has been raining steadily the last few days and has let up for the moment but I know that we had better work fast or we could be caught in a new downpour. I am getting Dee ready to ride her for the first time. We have done a lot of ground work already but she needs to be driven with the saddle on a few more times before we get on her back. I like to have them moving around pretty good with the driving line before we go to the next step. I attach the long black line to one side of the halter and, throwing the other end up on her back, I walk around and attach it on the other side of the halter. The line is about fifteen feet long, which puts me well behind her should she decide to kick out.

Dee has huge hips that look even bigger because she is not very tall. While she is quiet by nature, she is young enough to want to challenge me for the leadership role. She acts as if I am another horse that she needs to dominate.

Being careful not to wrap the line around my hand or get my feet caught up in it I cluck to her and tap her on her hip with the line asking her to go forward.

"No, I do not want to go into that puddle. I do not even see any dry spots,"

"What if there is something in the puddle that I can't see? No, nope not going there"

Dee is afraid and no matter how many times I ask she does not move her feet to go forward. I know there is nothing for her to be afraid so I talk to her quietly but firmly and keep asking her to move forward. No matter to her; I may know there is nothing to be afraid of but she doesn't and today is not a high-trust day on her part.

"Not going there!" she says.

I know if I slap her hip with the driving line hard enough that she will move forward but I also know that I am going to start a fight with her if I start out that way. When I challenge them to a fight I get one. When I am creative I can get them to do what I want without a fight, sometimes without their even being aware of it. Taking a few minutes to think about it I decide to pull her head first to the left and then to the right. By doing this she has to move her feet a few steps one way then another until pretty soon she has gone a good ten feet into the arena and has actually gotten her feet a little wet in a puddle. I continue to take her head left then right and she continues to move her feet and pretty soon we are in the middle of the arena.

"Well, I guess this isn't so bad after all."

"A little wet but the water isn't cold and it actually feels kind of good and nothing has hurt me yet."

"Hi there Karma, look at me, look at me. I walked all the way to the end of the arena, bet you can't do that!"

Dee is very pleased with herself. She walked through the puddles and to the end of the arena not once but three times before we were done.

INSIGHTS:

The mark of a great leader is her ability to step back from the situation at hand and use creative problem-solving rather than force to accomplish their goals. Great leaders never give up but instead will look for new methods to accomplish their goals knowing that using force will only alienate those they lead. Force evokes negative memories. Creative problem- solving evokes memories of achievement and self-confidence, ensuring that the individual feels good about his accomplishment and has learned the skill so that it can be repeated.

Jean and Sylk

CHAPTER 6

Riding Herd

⌐ INSPIRING FOLLOW-SHIP THROUGH FEEL

Indirect feel occurs when horses are out in the pasture or corral and you do not have any physical contact with them from a halter or snaffle bit but you still influence what they do. The horse can sense what a person wants him to do and will try to understand a person's intent. This indirect feel is powerful and can influence whether the horse wants to stay with you as his leader and what direction and speed he moves.

Refining your leadership skills is becoming so highly connected and tuned with the people you lead that you influence them to desire to follow you and choose you as their leader. You develop a mental and spiritual bonding with your followers.

*Your body is an
intelligent instrument;
learn to trust
what it tells you.*

⌒ Communicate with Balance

Even though the sun is already streaming down, the early
morning air is cool and Sylk is obviously invigorated. She
is happily galloping around in the arena. Her nostrils flare
when she snorts, blowing out air that at first glance reminds
me of gray thunder clouds as they circle, loop, and swirl.
Our famous Ellensburg wind whips, pulls, and pushes the
air, blowing her clouds of breath upward and away. Racing
toward us only to whirl around and lope off in the other
direction, Sylk is having fun and I know that the management team is beginning to wonder what on earth they have
gotten themselves into. I can see on their faces that they are
a little nervous watching Sylk. She can be very intimidat-
ing when she races around and slides to a stop in front of
you. Our first exercise for the day will be a demonstration
that I will do for them. Lifting my long black whip where it
is leaning on the barn wall, I walk into the round pen with
Sylk. The word *dance* tumbles and plays in my mind so I tell
them I am going to do a dance of communication with Sylk.

Their assignment is to look for leadership actions,
behaviors, and traits, both in my actions and Sylk's
responses.

To enter our dance I know that my first step is to
get her attention. I do that by positioning my body in the
middle of the pen and slightly in front of her. By placing
my body slightly in front of her I am telling her to stop and

look at me. There is no need for me to speak. She is very aware of my body and what it communicates. My stance is quiet but watchful and I wait for her to begin to look at me. A slight movement on my part and she is apt to take off galloping around again, so I stand and wait. Only when she is quiet and watching me do I begin to move her around the pen with my body movements. I speak occasionally but more for my benefit than hers as she reads what my body is telling her to do regardless of what I say. To demonstrate to the team I tell her "whoa, whoa" but at the same time I am moving the long black nylon end of the whip around behind her hindquarters. My nonverbal communication is more believable than my verbal commands, therefore she keeps trotting even though I am saying whoa.

She moves around the pen at a walk, then trot and lope, depending on the pressure and energy I apply with my body to her hindquarters. If I apply too much pressure then she takes off out of control again. Concentrating on her and the amount of energy I apply is very critical to the success of our dance. When I want her to slow down or change gaits I either increase or decrease my energy by slight movements. She reads the energy in my body, even the rate of my breath. With my focused energy and full attention on her, we are in sync and flow with no need to speak because I am communicating in her language.

After twenty minutes of "dance" I stop our demonstration so we can brainstorm the key traits of leadership as the Team saw them in the dance. They call out the key traits as they saw them and I write them on the white board. We whittle our list down to the following seven insights:

INSIGHTS:

- Effective leaders have patience; they know that quietness and having a wait attitude is important to their success.

- Effective leaders concentrate and focus on the immediate goal at hand.

- Effective leaders focus their attention on the people they lead.

- Effective leaders are aware that the level and consistency of the energy they display is important.

- Effective leaders speak in language that those they lead understand.

- Effective leaders know that their non-verbal communication is more believable than their verbal.

- Effective leaders know that communication is a physical action.

Snickers

⌒ Deliver the Right Cues

Towering over me when I stand next to him, Snicker's winter hair coat is the color of a dish of Oreo cookie ice cream. Around his belly the hair has come in thicker and darker while his shoulders are still a multi-colored white, brown, red, and black. Each new day he seems to grow taller. At almost two years old it is rare to have a western pleasure horse that stands almost six-feet tall in people terms and, I believe a prelude to how striking he will be in the show pen. His personality is that of a gentle giant even as a youngster and I know that the older he gets the quieter he will be. We are performing the ground work with him to get him ready to start under saddle in the next two months. We like for our young horses to have good ground manners and be trained to move away from pressure while completing several maneuvers on the ground before we ask for them under saddle. With the advent of fall the hills are truly alive with the colors red, green, brown, and gold. It's a beautiful time of year and time to finish up in some of our work with the young horses before winter sets in.

Most of our work at this stage of Snickers' training is executed in the round pen. First I begin our work today by asking him to walk around the pen to the left; letting him go about ten feet and then, using my body as the communication tool, I ask him to turn and walk to the right. Second, I increase the energy in my body, making a clucking noise with my mouth and ask him to jog trot. I notice that if I move my feet out of the center of the round pen even the slightest bit he increases his speed.

It is not always easy to see this type of finite communication with an older horse because they have learned how to tune humans out when needed. People are unaware that with their every move they are constantly communicating with the horse so they send all kinds of mixed messages with no follow-through so the horses learn to tune them out for self-preservation. However, with a young horse the subtleties of communication are more visibly seen if you are paying attention.

Because at this age everything I do with Snickers becomes a learning tool for him I want to be very clear with my body movements. At the same time Snickers is a little lazy so I find myself stepping out of the circle fairly often to keep him going in tempo. I am finding it a hard balance to keep as each time my feet move just slightly out of the circle he moves his body as close to the round pen wall as possible and speeds up. Nevertheless I attempt to maintain my posture in the center of the arena and move my feet only to rebalance myself.

Next, after Snickers has jogged around the pen several times, I bring my body energy up even more, make a kissing noise to him with my mouth, and ask him to lope. I turn him left then right a few times around the pen. At this faster gait I see that if I position my body barely behind his hindquarters he lopes faster. The slightest pressure to his hindquarters is a push to him and he thinks I want him to move into a faster gait. Backing off and moving back to the center of the pen causes him to slow his gait down a little. My pressure on his hindquarters must be balanced. Too much and he goes off running around the pen away from me, while too little and he decides to be lazy and stop to stare over the fence. All our communication heightens at his faster speed. He begins to feel too much pressure and gallops off paying no attention to me whatsoever. So I know that the pressure is too much too soon and I need to back off. Backing off and re-positioning myself in the middle of the circle causes Snickers to go back into his rocking lope.

Essentially it feels like having a push-button doll that I can maneuver with little effort on my part. After another few minutes of asking him to lope around the pen I see that he is uncomfortable with something and moving faster and closer to the wall than I want him to. Enjoying the play with him, I get even more watchful of my movements so that I can see what is causing his discomfort. I am amazed when I see that even if my hip sways to the side he takes this as communication. It takes me a few minutes to realize that this barest of movement on my part is the reason for his feeling uncomfortable and pressured.

I am feeling quite excited with this new-found information. It has huge implications for all my communications.

To conclude our work, I decide to bring him down to a walk and walk beside him around the pen. I do not halter him because I want him to become accustomed to me walking and then jogging beside him as a form of exercise for both of us. My senses are heightened so it does not take me long to see that as long as I stay right beside him matching my pace to his that we flow and are in sync. I get that feeling of being totally connected. It feels almost like an emotional high as we jog around and around.

However I feel so good about what we are accomplishing that I get excited and my pace starts to quicken and in a few steps I am now moving out in front of him. I can see that he is confused when I get too far in front of him so

I slow myself down, allowing him to catch up. One more time around and I find myself out in front again. This time I decide to play with him some so I keep going and pretty soon I am maybe four feet in front of him. Turning my head a little to see what he will do, I keep moving but he jogs to a standstill. I want to see if he will begin to jog again if I just keep going around, so I stay with it and go around about half the length of the pen. Snickers just stands and watches me. He is not sure what to do so he stays put. I stop jogging and go back to him and caress his shoulders lightly to connect up again. Staying close to his shoulders I cluck to him and ask for him to jog around once more. Because I want to see what he will do, I make sure that I stay in pace with him while we go around two times, then I begin to increase my pace. Three feet out in front of him, he stops in confusion and stands staring at me. I know now that pace and distance is very important in leading him and that if I get too far out in front of him I will lose him entirely.

Insights:

Leaders, you are always communicating. Even slight body movements or posture send messages to others. It is essential to your effectiveness as a leader to be aware of the messages you are sending.

Balanced pressure and timing are essential ingredients in reaching your goals. In your leadership efforts you will need to find the right balance of pressure to apply to get from point A to point B. Too little pressure and then the goal might not seem important enough and your team will take their focus off reaching the goal, while too much pressure will cause the person to feel frustrated and simply drop out. Timing in applying pressure is also a key component.

If your timing in applying the pressure is off, your efforts to effectively lead will be foiled.

All communication is heightened when you are moving at a faster speed. A faster speed increases stress and each communication is more intense. Slow-down may be needed for you to reach your goals.

Pace and distance are the next things to consider in your leadership efforts. Too far behind and you may be applying too much or too little pressure to be effective. Too far in front and you will lose your followers. When you get too far out in front your team members will become confused and not be sure how to reach the desired goals. You may know the steps and the pace but if you are so far in front that they feel left behind they will stall out and fall behind without clear instructions from you.

Riding the fence
will eventually
break the rail.

⌒ Provide More Praise Than Correction

Tasha, looking tall and regal, is growing her winter hair. She is a deep bay with some red tones to her coat where she got sun-bleached throughout the summer months. I lightly rub her hair crossways to how it lays and see that underneath her new hair is very dark, almost black, under her sun-bleached coat. I am very excited to see what she will look like after she gets in her new coat and then sheds it through the winter. I brush her and spend some time just hanging out with her and then it's time to begin work.

I start her out by putting a snaffle bit in her mouth that has a long rein. Then standing to her left side just in front of her hip I pull the rein to the left. I am asking her to give her head and neck to me by applying pressure to the rein and holding it until she gives and puts her nose to her side. I do this four or five times, each time waiting until she has given me her head which releases the pressure on the rein. As soon as she gives to the pressure I drop the rein like it is a hot potato. Release is what teaches her she has done what I have asked, so I want to be very clear and quick with the release once she has given to the rein pressure. Rubbing her hip with my free hand, "good girl, good girl," I tell her in a quiet soothing tone. She may not understand the words but she understands the tone and the release of the pressure so she knows she has done well. Satisfied with her response on the left side I move around to her right side and repeat the process. Once she is giving to the rein pressure I know it is time to move on to the next step.

"Tasha, what a good girl you are." I caress her shoulders and down her back. She is very relaxed as she licks her lips and looks around at me.

Next I ask her to bend her head and neck around to me and then using my index finger I apply pressure to her side just in front of her hip. I want her to move away from my finger by moving her hip over and side stepping around with her feet. This disengages her hindquarters and sets us up for more maneuvers down the road. If she gets slow and sluggish I tap her hip with the end of the rein to get her to move off the pressure. I want her to get used to moving away from light pressure. When she moves away from my finger, I rub her to a stop so the last thing she feels is the relaxing rub of my hand on her hip. After we have finished this several times on the left side I move around and repeat the process on the right side. She is very responsive today so in ten minutes we have completed our exercises on the ground. Today is not the first day we have worked on these bends and moving her hip from the pressure of my finger. These have been rituals since she was a yearling so now by her late two-year-old year she knows what to do and does it willingly.

The first exercise of getting her to give her neck and head to pressure sets us up to move to the next exercise of disengaging her hip and moving off the pressure of my finger. Both of these exercises will help with our riding work as I will be asking the same thing from her. Only then when I ask for her to move her hip around it will be with my heel. Each exercise builds on the next and we do not move on to the next exercise until she is satisfactorily completing the one before that. With the completion of each exercise, praise and release from pressure are key components before we move on.

We complete the exercise; I release her from pressure, praise and caress her, and then put her back into her stall. If we try to do too much in any one session she will get nervous and frustrated. Taking it slow and easy and building on each step ensures a successful work session and in the end a trained horse who is willing to do as I ask. She is learning to trust that I will not ask too much of her in any one session and is beginning to feel confidence in herself that she is able to do her job.

INSIGHTS:

Effective leaders use a building strategy. Leadership is having the knowledge and vision of the big picture with the skills and abilities to break down the big picture into many small pictures. The small pictures have a series of goals and objectives which, when completed, successfully will add up to the whole, the completion of the big-picture vision. To accomplish the vision effective leaders ask those they lead for small, achievable steps giving praise and encouragement for reaching each goal. Leading in this way builds trust and self-confidence in your team.

When an individual is learning a new skill the same philosophy applies. Ask for small, achievable steps, giving praise after each success. Asking for too much too soon just creates overwhelm and leads to failure. By building on each successful step people will gain confidence in their ability to perform their tasks, feeling good about their efforts and increase their belief in you as a leader who knows how to lead. This environment is a win-win for both parties.

Great leaders
know how to make the
right thing easy and the
wrong thing hard.

⌒ Influence Tactfully and Consistently

Snickers is wandering around inside the round pen, occasionally sticking his head over the top bar to look off longingly into the pasture. The pen is six-feet tall but he has grown so tall over the summer that he can stick his neck over and hang his head on the top rung. His eyes are big and quiet, and with the black on his head along with the white strip down his face he is breathtaking in his beauty. I am sure he would rather go out and eat in the pasture but when Cliff goes into the pen, he turns and looks at him as if to say: "Okay, I am ready. Let's go."

Cliff puts him into a walk, then jog around the pen. Using the lunge whip as an extension of his arm he asks him to jog around a few steps then turns him around to go the other way with his body positioning. After a few minutes of this exercise he has Snickers' attention on him. He asks Snickers to increase his gait to a lope by kissing to him with his mouth, increasing the energy in his body and extending the whip out. Snickers goes into a nice rocking lope around the pen.

Cliff wants to teach him to turn, back up, and walk forward with Cliff behind him giving cues with the driving line. We do this exercise with him before we begin to saddle and ride him. We also use this exercise with our other horses as a way of getting them soft in the bit and softly moving away from pressure. Hooking up the driving line which is really a long rope with snaps at the end, to the left and right side of Snickers' halter, he asks him to walk around the round pen. He taps him on his hindquarters to get him going and then, walking behind him about ten feet, he walks him around one way then another. When Snickers is moving around easy and quiet, which only takes about twenty minutes, it is time to move on to the next step.

The round pen is just that, a round pen with aluminum panels that are attached together to form a fifty-foot circle. This aluminum panel circle gives the horse a wall of sorts as a boundary or barrier. What I have noticed is that the horses begin to get comfortable with the wall and use it as a self-imposed boundary. They feel safe inside this wall because they are enclosed in a small area. The problem comes when you stay inside this small area with them so much that they begin to rely on the wall as support. Then they get very nervous and afraid when you take them out to the larger arena.

Cliff is ready to move Snickers into the arena which is eighty by one-hundred-thirty feet. Snickers gets very nervous in the bigger arena and gets resistant to the driving line. His eyes are big and his body stiffens. He attempts to avoid walking forward. Cliff has to encourage him over and over, by talking softly to him, then tapping him on his hindquarters with the line. Snickers takes a few steps forward and then stalls out. Cliff kisses to him again, talks to him, and pushes him forward. Over and over again he repeats this until Snickers has gone around the arena two or three laps. By now he is getting quieter and feeling more secure in the big area and surer that nothing in this new space will hurt him. Cliff stays with him and drives him one more lap around, then removes the driving line and leads him around the arena talking to him the whole time.

Snickers is quiet and at ease and lowers his head and licks his lips to show his acceptance.

INSIGHTS:

Effective leaders recognize their own self -imposed boundaries and consistently move these boundaries further and further out. Only in expanding our self-imposed boundaries do we continue to grow personally and professionally.

Individuals establish their own sets of boundaries or barriers. They too will become comfortable in their space and feel fear and uncertainty in moving out of this space. It is up to their leader to recognize these barriers and the fears that cause them to attempt to stay within these barriers. Inspiring follow-ship means guiding the person one step at a time through these boundaries and then staying with them until they are comfortable enough to walk on alone. In this way, the person is continually enlarging his comfort zone and taking on more and more challenges.

Tasha

⁓ Lead with Soft Eyes

Cupid is racing around the arena kicking his heels in the air and the white star on his black face looks like a beacon beckoning to me. He streaks by me bucking and kicking. He is having fun running a few feet from his dam, Bell, and then running back to her and poking his nose into her hind-quarters, hiding under her tail. His hair coat is a blue roan color and when he streaks around and around he truly looks almost blue which is a rare and sought-after color. He is a three-month-old quarter horse colt and today we are planning to lead him around the arena so that he can get used to the lead line and halter. This is his first leading lesson.

Cliff quietly walks up to Bell and waits until Cupid is close enough to him so that he can put his arms around his chest and hold him. Working quickly but softly I slip the halter on Cupid's head and buckle it up. Then I snap a lead rope to the halter. Cliff takes hold of Cupid's lead rope while I snap another lead rope onto Bell's halter. Now that we have a lead rope on both Bell and Cupid we are ready to lead them around the arena.

I tug lightly on Bell's halter and ask her to walk beside me. Cliff tries to stay up with Cupid when he takes off running to catch up with Bell. I slow my pace so that Cliff can catch up with us. Cupid comes to a standstill and refuses to move forward. Cliff pulls on the lead rope, attempting to move him forward, but Cupid plants his feet and refuses to move. Cliff pulls on him again but Cupid keeps his feet planted and Cliff ends up pulling his face forward and out. Cupid does not intend to move his feet. Cliff keeps pulling but all he ends up doing is pulling Cupid so that his feet slide in the arena. So while he gets him to move, it is all by force and Cupid is resisting the whole way.

Next, to help Cliff out, we take a long lead rope and put it behind Cupid's hindquarters so that Cliff is holding one end of the rope and I have the other end. In this way we can push on his hindquarters at the same time Cliff is pulling on the lead rope attached to his halter. In this way we create a push–pull effect in our attempt to lead Cupid. Cupid keeps the lead rope on his halter tight by continuing to keep his feet planted. When we push on his hindquarters, Cliff and I both pulling at the same time against him with the rope, all we accomplish is sliding him forward a few steps. Our hands are getting tired so we decide to try something new. Dropping the lead rope off his hindquarters, Cliff pulls Cupid's head first left then right, applying enough pressure to get his feet to move. It's not long until Cupid is moving forward without even knowing it. Cliff creates a see-saw effect when he pulls his head left then right. We can see that pushing or pulling him is not going to work. Using his forward movement as he runs to stay up with Bell, we walk around and around the arena. This teaches him to get accustomed to the lead rope and halter as along with someone walking beside him.

Next I hold Bell in place while Cliff moves Cupid slightly left and right to get him to move a few steps at a time away from Bell. Having made some progress we decide that Cupid has had enough for today.

Over the next two or three months we work daily with Cupid for short periods of time each day. Spending time with him and Bell, leading them both as well as brushing them and establishing a connection by simply being with them, we eventually are able to lead him around the arena while Bell stays put. When the time comes we wean him from Bell and continue with his lessons on his own.

Now a few months later he allows me to halter him and lead him around by himself. So today I halter him and lead him out to the round pen for an hour of exercise and play. When I walk him out of the barn to the round pen I expect him to walk beside me with his head in line with my shoulder. If he gets ahead of me I turn him around in a circle which slows him down naturally and brings him back to the correct position beside me. I neither pull him nor push him to get him to walk beside me. Instead I guide him in the direction I want him to go. The lead rope I carry in my hands is weightless. Cupid walks beside me with his weight balanced equally on his four feet. His shoulders are up and he is using his hindquarters. He carries his body upright and straight. I guide him in the direction I want to go by the movement of my body and my verbal commands. He has self-carriage and is choosing to be guided by me out of respect and trust which has been established by many hours of companionship and work.

INSIGHTS:

Great leadership is having the ability to guide those you lead by feel. Guiding by feel means you have established an emotional connection where the individuals know, trust, and respect you as their leader. Using all your senses you feel the connection and know when you have a flow and when something is amiss. You are guiding with a touch that is so light it feels weightless, light, and airy while exceptionally strong. The connection is like an unbreakable cord that is invisible to the naked eye. But you sense and feel it. Therefore you know when it is stretched and needs attention. Leadership by feel is neither a push nor a pull but a guide. There can be no force in weightlessness. Tom Dorrance, largely considered the father of natural horsemanship, talks about this weightlessness when working with a horse is his book True Horsemanship Through Feel. This "Feel" is difficult to understand and even more difficult to attain but once you have the feel in your leadership efforts you know and love it. You understand that leadership on this higher plane offers a closer connection, a more unified effort, is more fun, and gives you and your team not only the capabilities to meet your goals but to exceed these goals. Once you experience leadership at this higher level you will always seek this higher plane of leadership, recognizing that true feel like other great aspirations is a progression and will differ with each individual.

⌐ Conclusion

I used the word Spirit in relationship to horses and leadership to signify our highest desire, motivation, and ability to go beyond acceptable to extraordinary.

Spirit symbolizes the horse: liberated, free, beautiful, and totally happy to be who they are. They have no need to compare themselves to others and come up short and neither do we. The spirit of the horse is unique and powerful just like each of us is unique and powerful. When we listen to our Spirit we become the person we were truly born to be. The messages that we are able to obtain from the horses are deep, powerful, and wonderfully freeing.

It is my desire that you will have obtained even one nugget of truth for yourself by reading this book. Horses and nature have much to share with us if we take the time to listen and learn.

Leadership takes many forms. You may be the leader of your family, the leader in your office, a political leader, the leader in your circle of friends, a church leader, or a girl- or boy-scout leader. You may be a group leader in the corporate arena or you may be a manager in a corporate or non-profit organization. You may be a coach or a consulting manager or you may just want to know more about leading yourself. Regardless of how you use your leadership abilities the first prerequisite is the willingness to grow yourself. In observing great leaders in their respective fields the thing that I have been most impressed with is that you cannot be a great leader without continual personal development. Great leaders are always growing and evolving because their leadership abilities are always in demand in new realms.

To be an effective leader we are always in process and we never arrive. But it is imperative that we all continue to walk down the trail of learning and self- discovery. The world continues to move around us and if we stand still then we are really going backwards. I hope you will choose to continue to grow. I know that this is the choice I have made.

Allow your spirit
to break free
and gallop
to your sunset!

97 Essential Actions to Lead with Spirit

1. Commit yourself to inspire follow-ship

2. Identify your emotions

3. Develop inner-harmony

4. Continue learning and improving yourself

5. Challenge yourself to move out your self imposed boundaries

6. Get quiet and listen

7. Manage your emotions and actions

8. Know whose energy is speaking

9. Learn to trust your body

10. Look deeply into yourself

11. Heal your own emotional wounds

12. Use and trust your intuition

13. Identify the true motives behind your actions

14. Perform self reflection

15. Guide with thoughts, feelings and actions

16. Be honest with yourself about your true intentions

17. Practice authentic behavior

18. Acknowledge your emotions

19. Center yourself

20. Exercise Self Confidence

21. Learn from past and emerging Leaders

22. Show presence and self carriage

23. Know how your style of leadership affects others

24. Be Flexible: Change methods as needed

25. Understand and respect diverse styles

26. Identify the individual's driving needs

27. Take time to reach the unreachable

28. See the possibilities

29. Be other focused

30. Lead both sides of the brain

31. Move forward with energy

32. Know when to allow for rest

33. Back up – balance and regroup as necessary

34. Be sensitive to their pressure points

35. Know where you are going before you leave the start gate

36. Give specific instructions

37. Value Instinct in your group

38. Put following you on auto pilot

39. Be sensitive to your groups "sensors"

40. Maintain a Positive Atmosphere

41. Be aware of external influences to your group

42. Form Partnerships

43. Take social needs into account

44. Understand team dynamics

45. Execute right pairing

46. Find intuitive flow

47. Develop your vision

48. Gain attention and respect

49. Connect and build trust

50. Build and maintain Relationship

51. Ask daily for the leadership role

52. Follow Through

53. Respect yourself and require respect from others

54. Connect emotionally

55. Value their trust

56. Show empathy

57. Validate their feelings

58. Make personal sacrifices for the team

59. Show respect for their needs

60. Lead to their natural strengths

61. Allow them to grow without protecting

62. Give them the chance to choose what is right for them

63. Forgive yourself for your miscalculations

64. Trust them to do it

65. Share yourself to build a firm foundation

66. Build trust by being open

67. Let go of control

68. Show up and be there in mind, body, and spirit
69. Send Clear focused Messages

70. Stay connected to your team

71. Make the right thing easy and the wrong
    thing hard

72. Give them the chance to do it right

73. Teach skills that will be used for a lifetime

74. Create opportunities for physical memory at the
    body level

75. Step them through their fears

76. Allow for feeling the fear

77. Take a step by step approach to overcoming fear

78. Expect 100% try

79. Develop strength of character

80. Identify the specific goal before you engage

81. Keep going till you reach your goal

82. Manage your energy to the situation

83. Creatively problem solve

84. Improvise rather than give up

85. Focus your attention and actions

86. Identify your non verbal cues

87. Speak in their language

88. Find the right balance of pressure and timing

89. Exercise the correct pace and distance

90. Know the messages you are sending

91. Use a building strategy

92. Ask for small achievable steps

93. Apply and release pressure appropriately

94. Guide them to expand their self imposed boundaries

95. Eliminate pulling or pushing and Guide by Feel

96. Walk alongside

97. Give more praise than correction

⌒ About the Author

For twenty years Jean Starling worked as a manager, team leader and consultant in the manufacturing and high technology industries implementing new business processes, managing client relationships and organizational development. She has worked with well known companies such as Oracle and Clarify Software. Along the way she earned an MBA degree with an emphasis on International Business.

Her love for horses finally led Jean and her husband, Cliff, to buy a ranch where, for the past ten years, their focus has been on raising, breeding, and producing show quality quarter horses.

Jean's life-long study of people took a new path as she began exploring how working with horses was allowing her to uncover truths about leadership in a new and interesting way.

Her more casual observations took an unexpected turn after the death of a family member when Jean discovered the keen sense horses have to read non-verbal body language and energy. They reacted to her grief by not responding to usual commands, reacting instead to a deeper sense of what she was really projecting. Observing her horses' responses allowed her to work through her emotional trauma and increased her understanding for the potential of horse/human interactions for people facing leadership challenges in their own lives.

Jean remains a passionate 'people whisperer' and she now uses this unique ability to work with horses to help executives, community leaders, and business entrepreneurs take their leadership skills and understanding to new levels.

For more information about Jean or working with her and her horses, please visit www.taking-the-reins.com.

Printed in the United States
74337LV00001B/161-254